CHEWBACCA AND THE SLAVERS OF THE SHADOWLANDS

Script **Chris Cerasi**

Art **Jennifer L. Meyer**

Lettering **Michael Heisler**

Cover **Jennifer L. Meyer**

Dark Horse Books®

**THIS STORY BEGINS APPROXIMATELY
SIX MONTHS AFTER THE BATTLE OF YAVIN.**

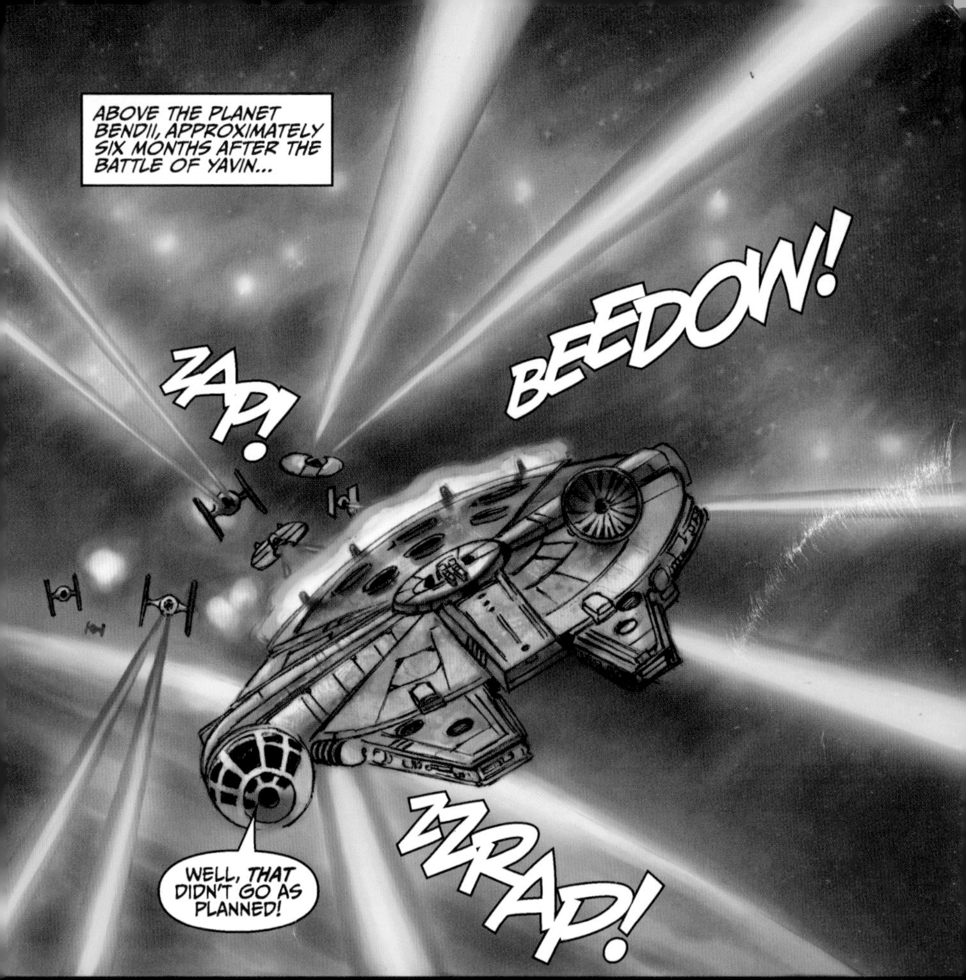
ABOVE THE PLANET BENDII, APPROXIMATELY SIX MONTHS AFTER THE BATTLE OF YAVIN...
ZAP!
BEEDOW!
WELL, *THAT* DIDN'T GO AS PLANNED!
ZZRAP!

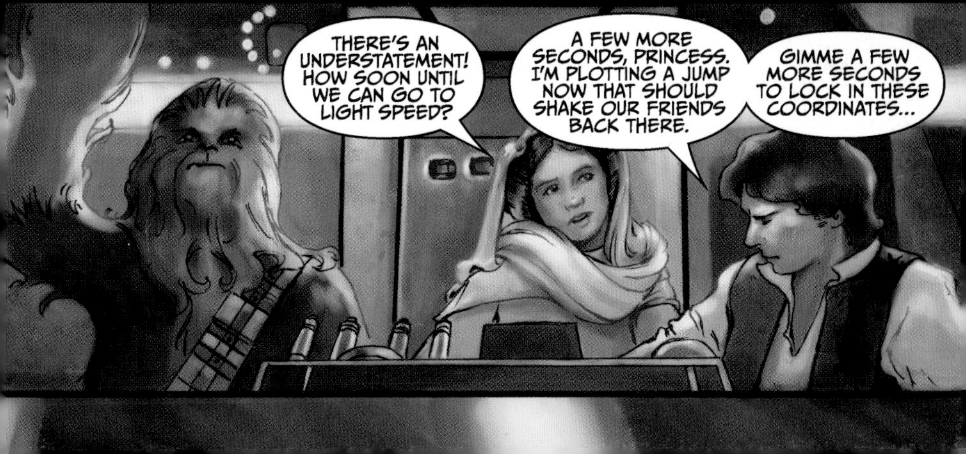
THERE'S AN UNDERSTATEMENT! HOW SOON UNTIL WE CAN GO TO LIGHT SPEED?
A FEW MORE SECONDS, PRINCESS. I'M PLOTTING A JUMP NOW THAT SHOULD SHAKE OUR FRIENDS BACK THERE.
GIMME A FEW MORE SECONDS TO LOCK IN THESE COORDINATES...

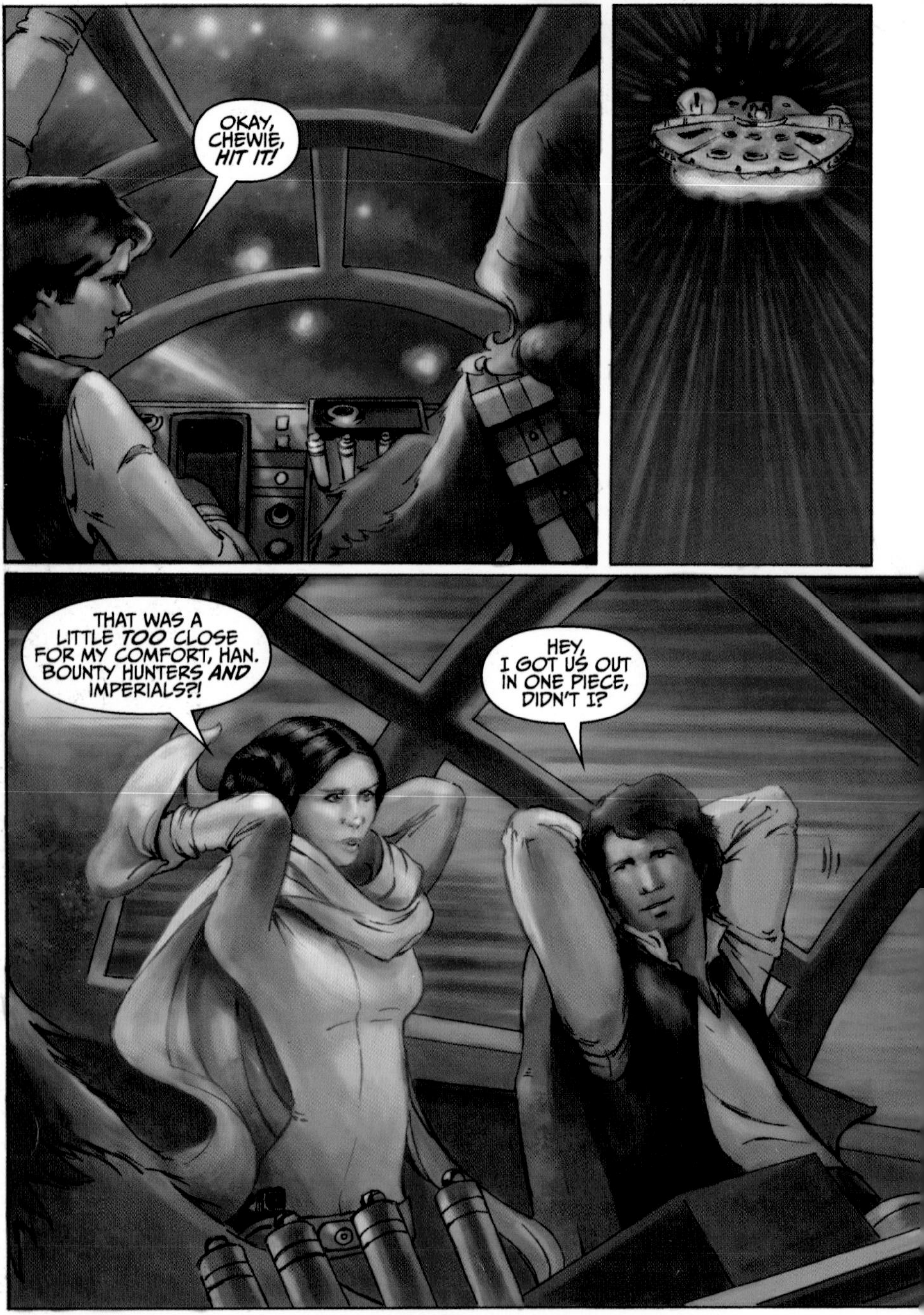
OKAY, CHEWIE, HIT IT!
THAT WAS A LITTLE TOO CLOSE FOR MY COMFORT, HAN. BOUNTY HUNTERS AND IMPERIALS?!
HEY, I GOT US OUT IN ONE PIECE, DIDN'T I?

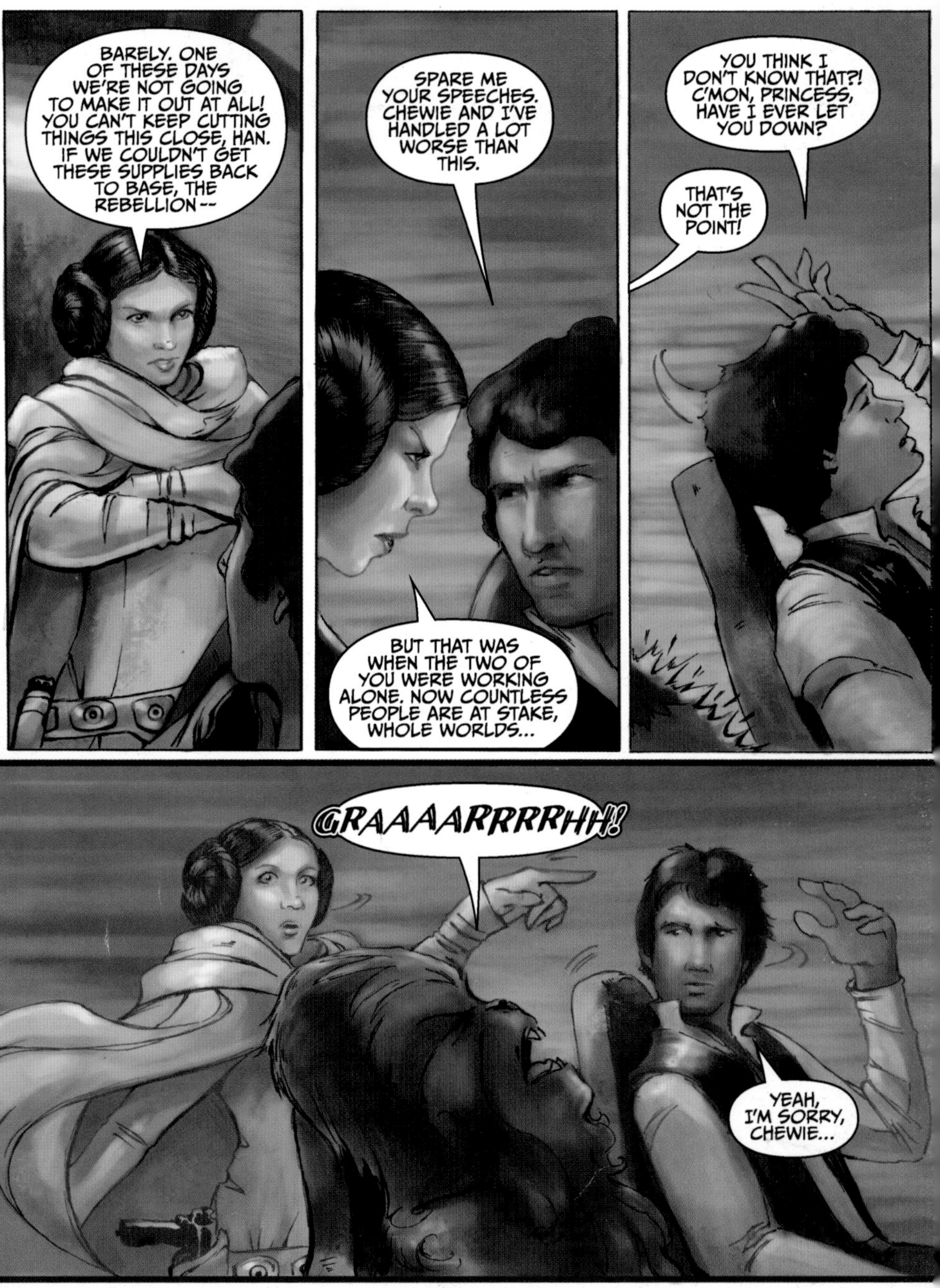

BARELY. ONE OF THESE DAYS WE'RE NOT GOING TO MAKE IT OUT AT ALL! YOU CAN'T KEEP CUTTING THINGS THIS CLOSE, HAN. IF WE COULDN'T GET THESE SUPPLIES BACK TO BASE, THE REBELLION--
SPARE ME YOUR SPEECHES. CHEWIE AND I'VE HANDLED A LOT WORSE THAN THIS.
BUT THAT WAS WHEN THE TWO OF YOU WERE WORKING ALONE. NOW COUNTLESS PEOPLE ARE AT STAKE, WHOLE WORLDS...
YOU THINK I DON'T KNOW THAT?! C'MON, PRINCESS, HAVE I EVER LET YOU DOWN?
THAT'S NOT THE POINT!
GRAAAARRRRHH!
YEAH, I'M SORRY, CHEWIE...

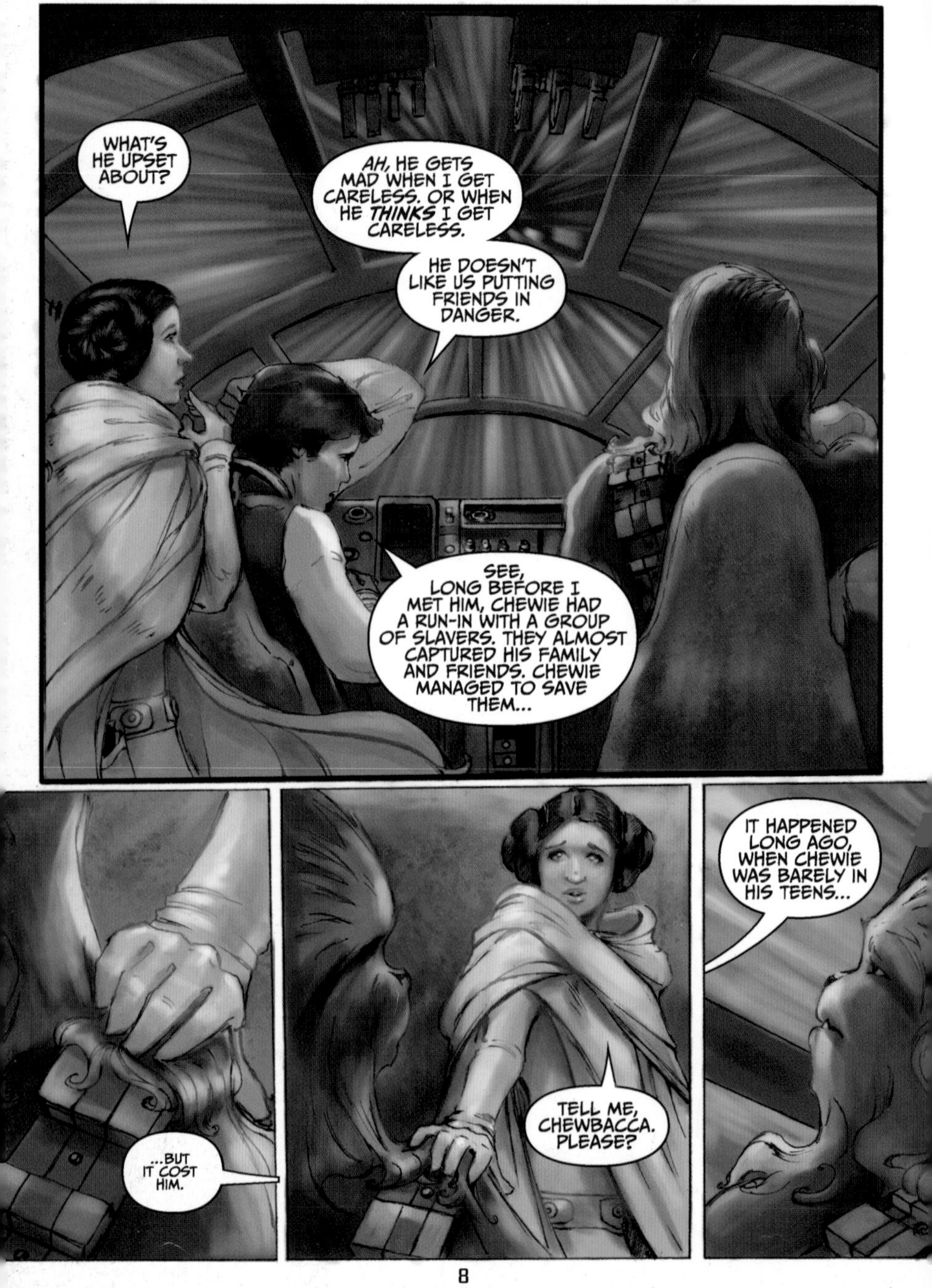
WHAT'S HE UPSET ABOUT?
AH, HE GETS MAD WHEN I GET CARELESS. OR WHEN HE ***THINKS*** I GET CARELESS.
HE DOESN'T LIKE US PUTTING FRIENDS IN DANGER.
SEE, LONG BEFORE I MET HIM, CHEWIE HAD A RUN-IN WITH A GROUP OF SLAVERS. THEY ALMOST CAPTURED HIS FAMILY AND FRIENDS. CHEWIE MANAGED TO SAVE THEM...
...BUT IT COST HIM.
TELL ME, CHEWBACCA. PLEASE?
IT HAPPENED LONG AGO, WHEN CHEWIE WAS BARELY IN HIS TEENS...

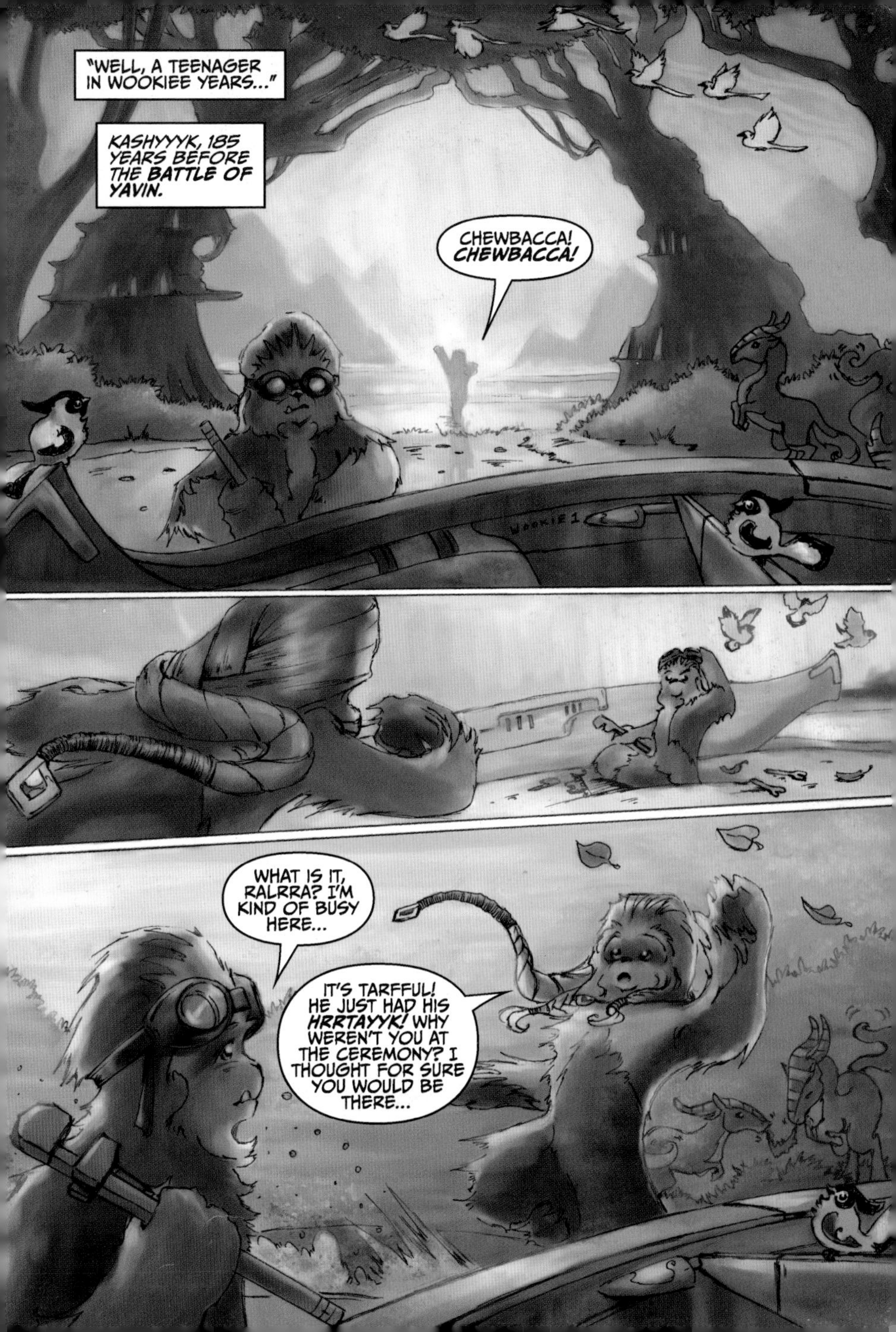
"WELL, A TEENAGER IN WOOKIEE YEARS..."
KASHYYYK, 185 YEARS BEFORE THE BATTLE OF YAVIN.
CHEWBACCA! CHEWBACCA!
WOOKIE 1
WHAT IS IT, RALRRA? I'M KIND OF BUSY HERE...
IT'S TARFFUL! HE JUST HAD HIS HRRTAYYK! WHY WEREN'T YOU AT THE CEREMONY? I THOUGHT FOR SURE YOU WOULD BE THERE...

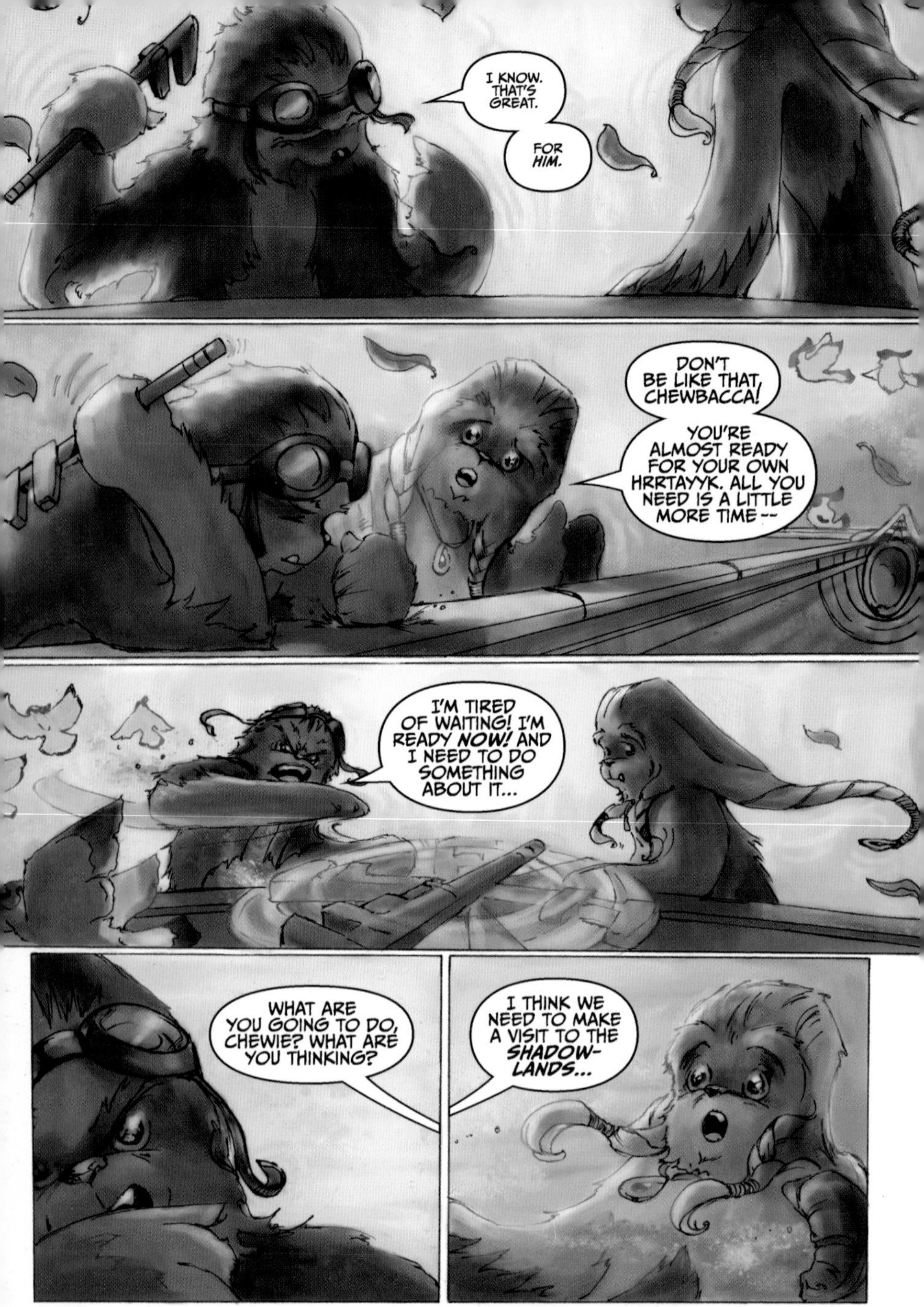

I KNOW. THAT'S GREAT.
FOR *HIM.*
DON'T BE LIKE THAT, CHEWBACCA!
YOU'RE ALMOST READY FOR YOUR OWN HRRTAYYK. ALL YOU NEED IS A LITTLE MORE TIME --
I'M TIRED OF WAITING! I'M READY *NOW!* AND I NEED TO DO SOMETHING ABOUT IT...
WHAT ARE YOU GOING TO DO, CHEWIE? WHAT ARE YOU THINKING?
I THINK WE NEED TO MAKE A VISIT TO THE *SHADOW-LANDS...*

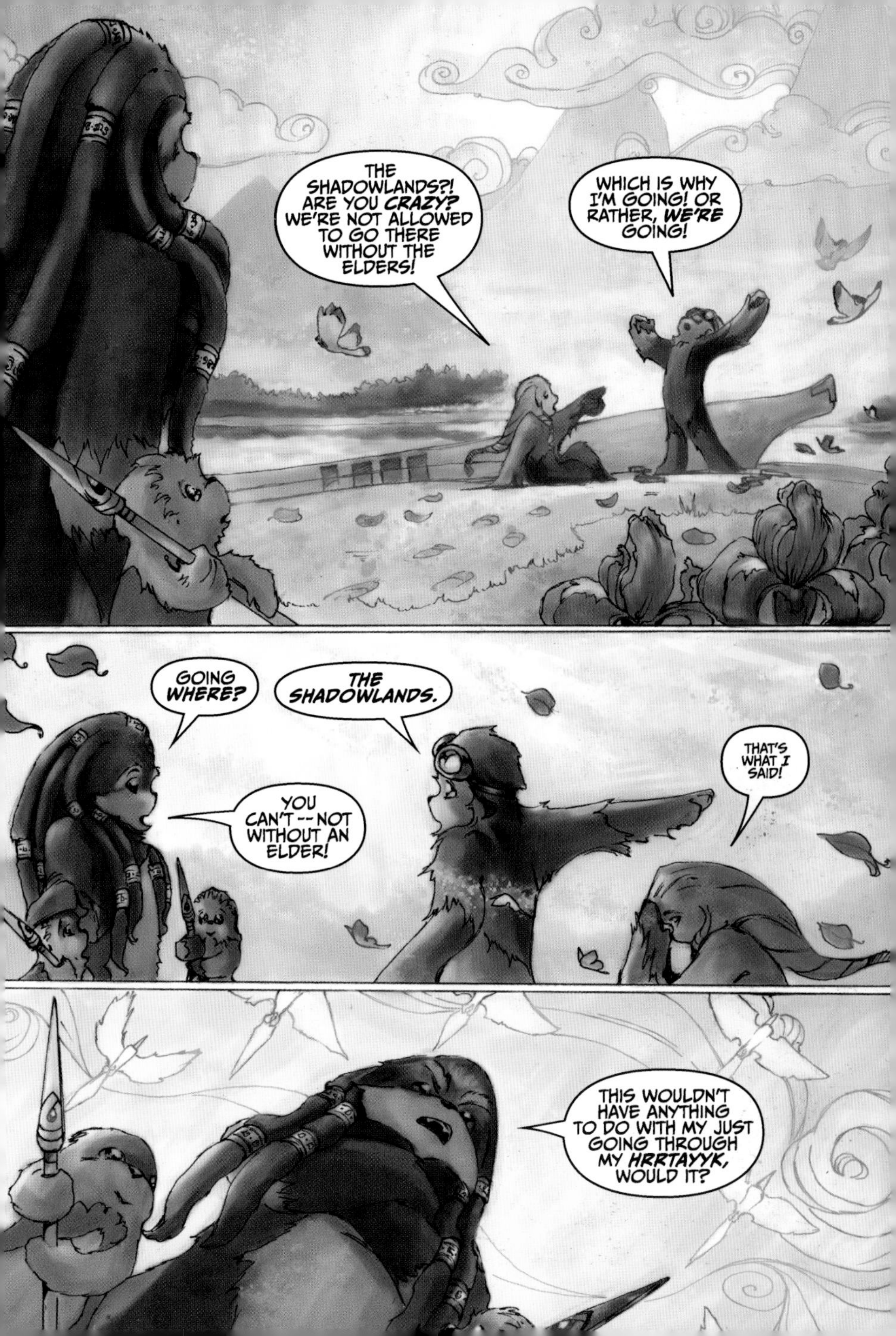
THE SHADOWLANDS?! ARE YOU CRAZY? WE'RE NOT ALLOWED TO GO THERE WITHOUT THE ELDERS!
WHICH IS WHY I'M GOING! OR RATHER, WE'RE GOING!
GOING WHERE?
THE SHADOWLANDS.
YOU CAN'T -- NOT WITHOUT AN ELDER!
THAT'S WHAT I SAID!
THIS WOULDN'T HAVE ANYTHING TO DO WITH MY JUST GOING THROUGH MY HRRTAYYK, WOULD IT?

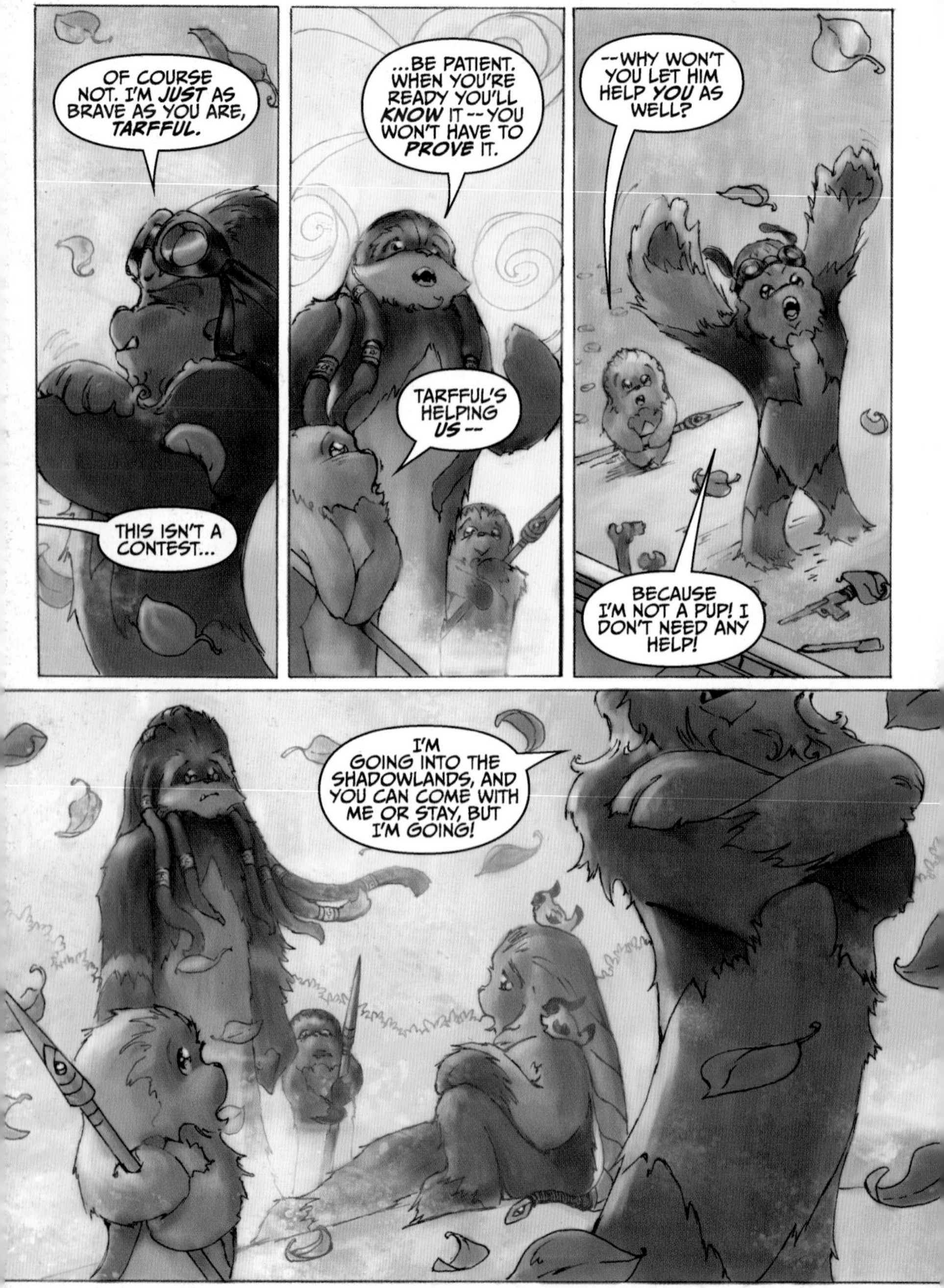
OF COURSE NOT. I'M *JUST* AS BRAVE AS YOU ARE, *TARFFUL.*
THIS ISN'T A CONTEST...
...BE PATIENT. WHEN YOU'RE READY YOU'LL *KNOW* IT -- YOU WON'T HAVE TO *PROVE* IT.
TARFFUL'S HELPING *US* --
--WHY WON'T YOU LET HIM HELP *YOU* AS WELL?
BECAUSE I'M NOT A PUP! I DON'T NEED ANY HELP!
I'M GOING INTO THE SHADOWLANDS, AND YOU CAN COME WITH ME OR STAY, BUT I'M GOING!

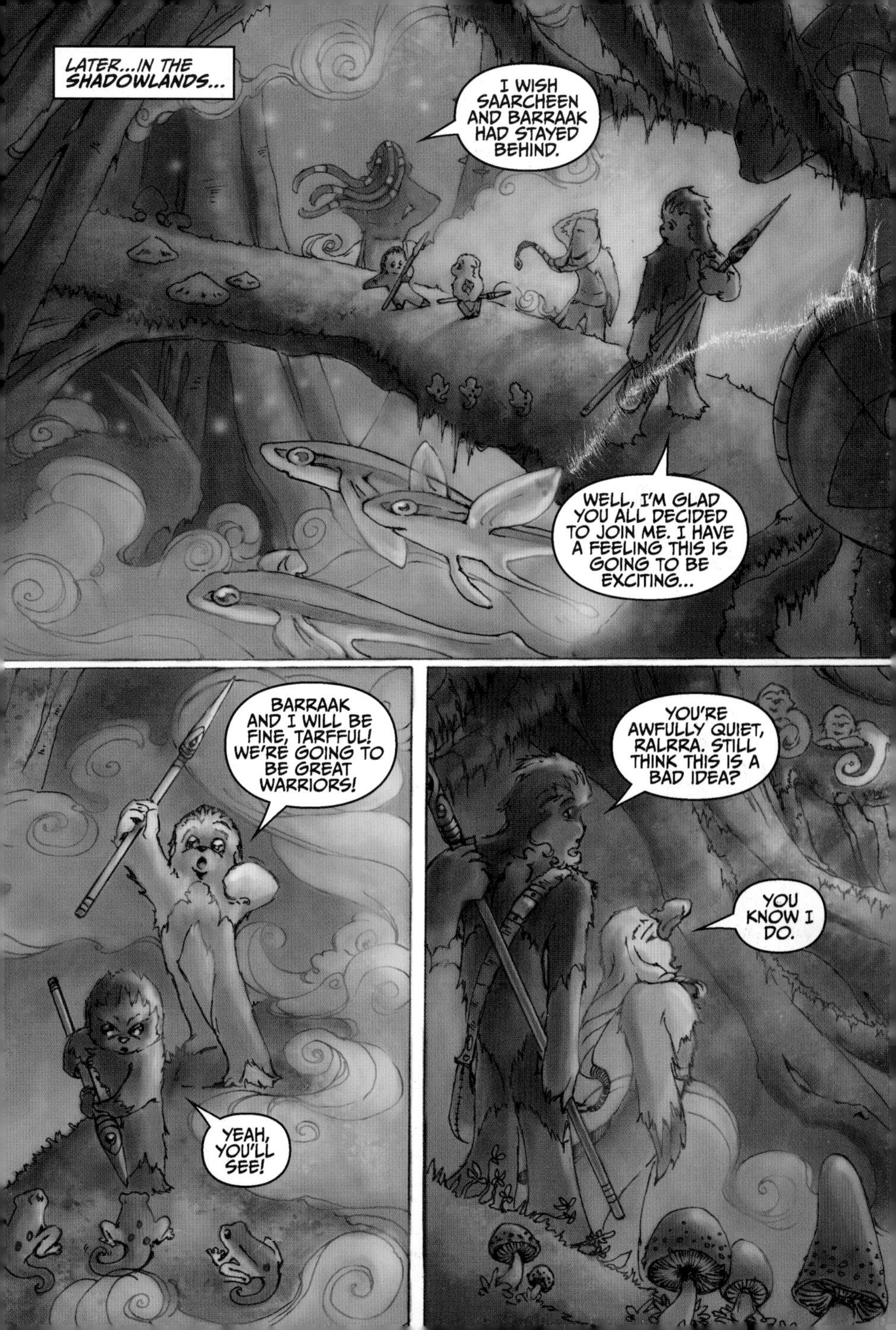
LATER...IN THE SHADOWLANDS...
I WISH SAARCHEEN AND BARRAAK HAD STAYED BEHIND.
WELL, I'M GLAD YOU ALL DECIDED TO JOIN ME. I HAVE A FEELING THIS IS GOING TO BE EXCITING...
BARRAAK AND I WILL BE FINE, TARFFUL! WE'RE GOING TO BE GREAT WARRIORS!
YEAH, YOU'LL SEE!
YOU'RE AWFULLY QUIET, RALRRA. STILL THINK THIS IS A BAD IDEA?
YOU KNOW I DO.

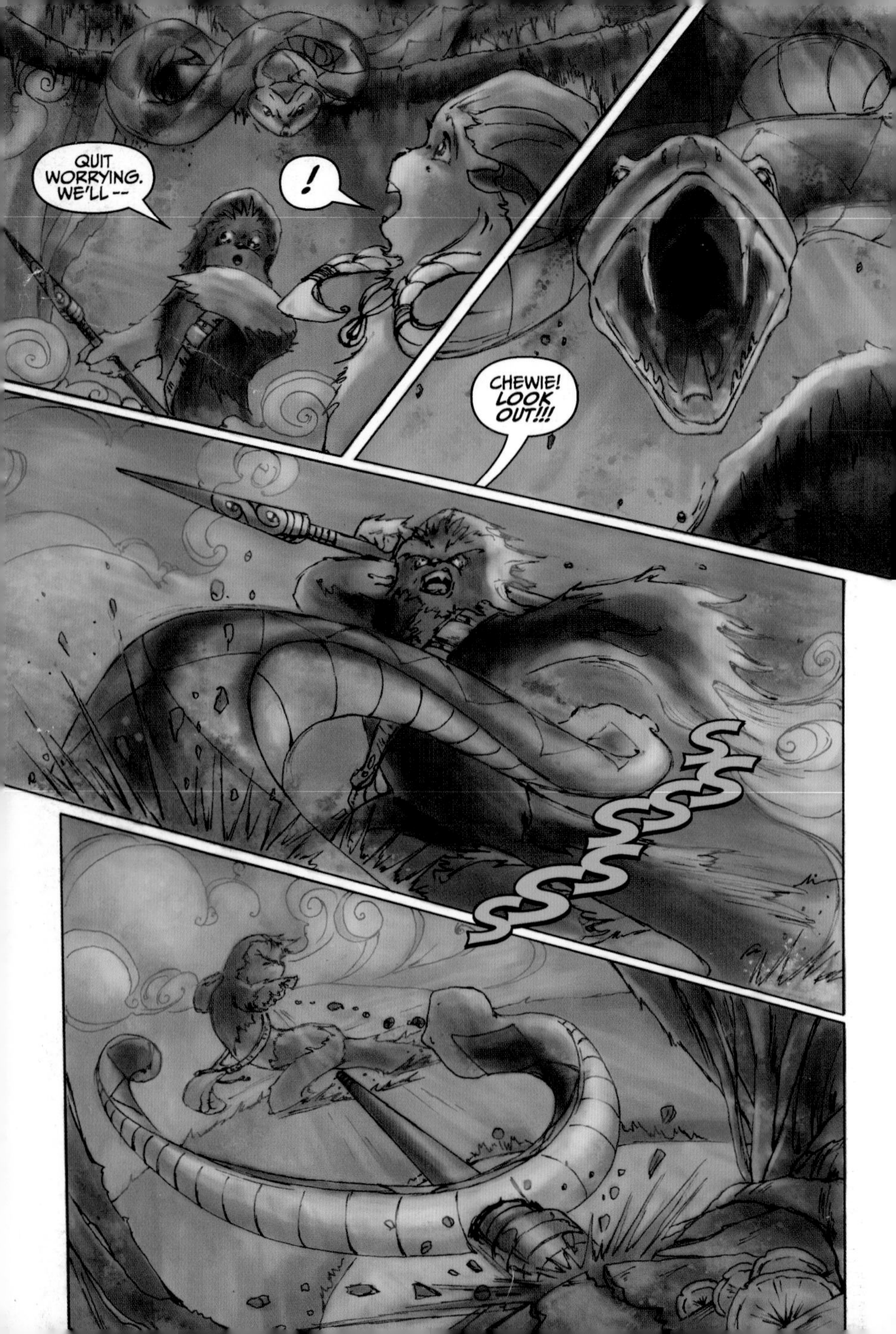
QUIT WORRYING. WE'LL --
!
CHEWIE! LOOK OUT!!!
SSSSSSS

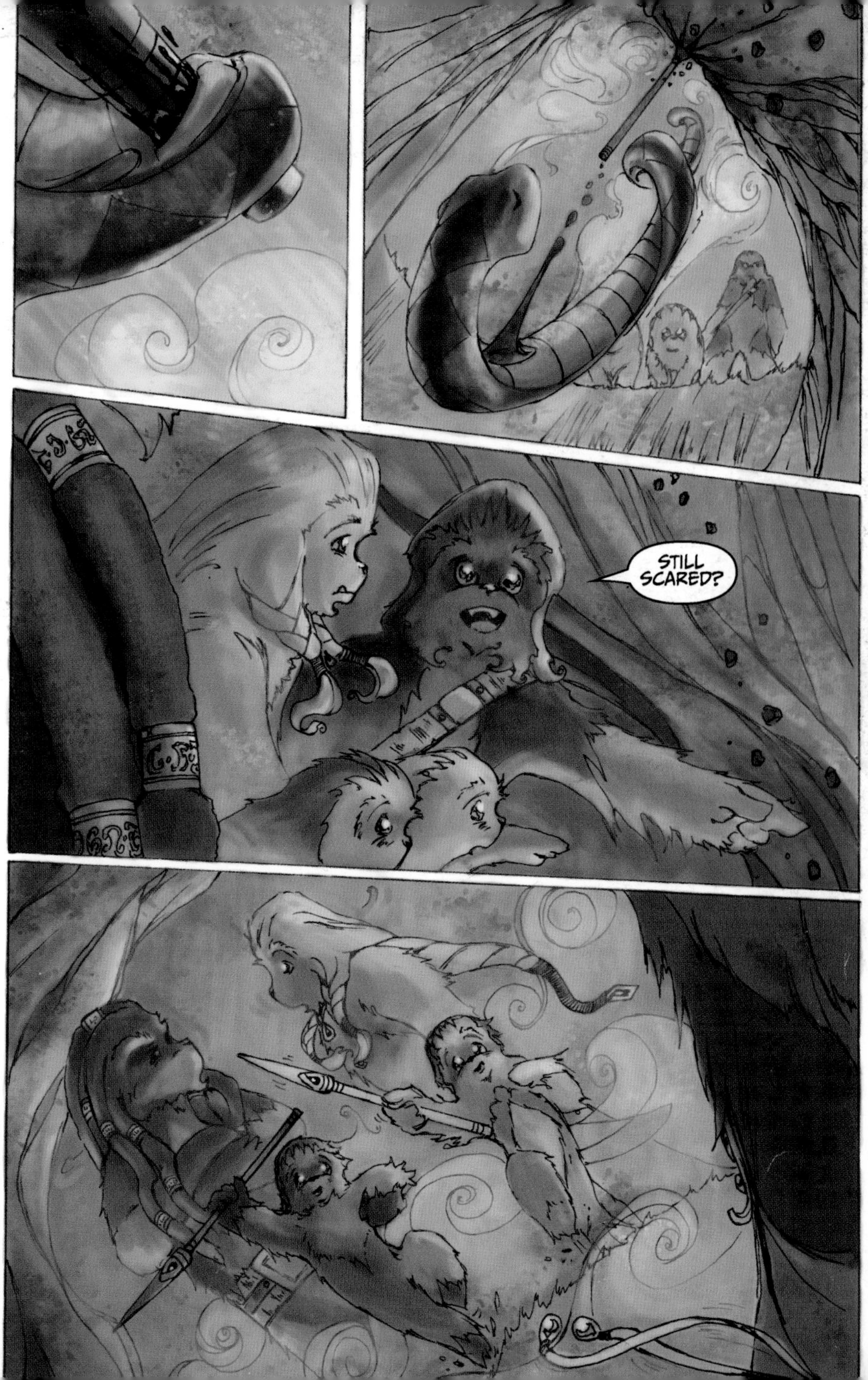
STILL SCARED?

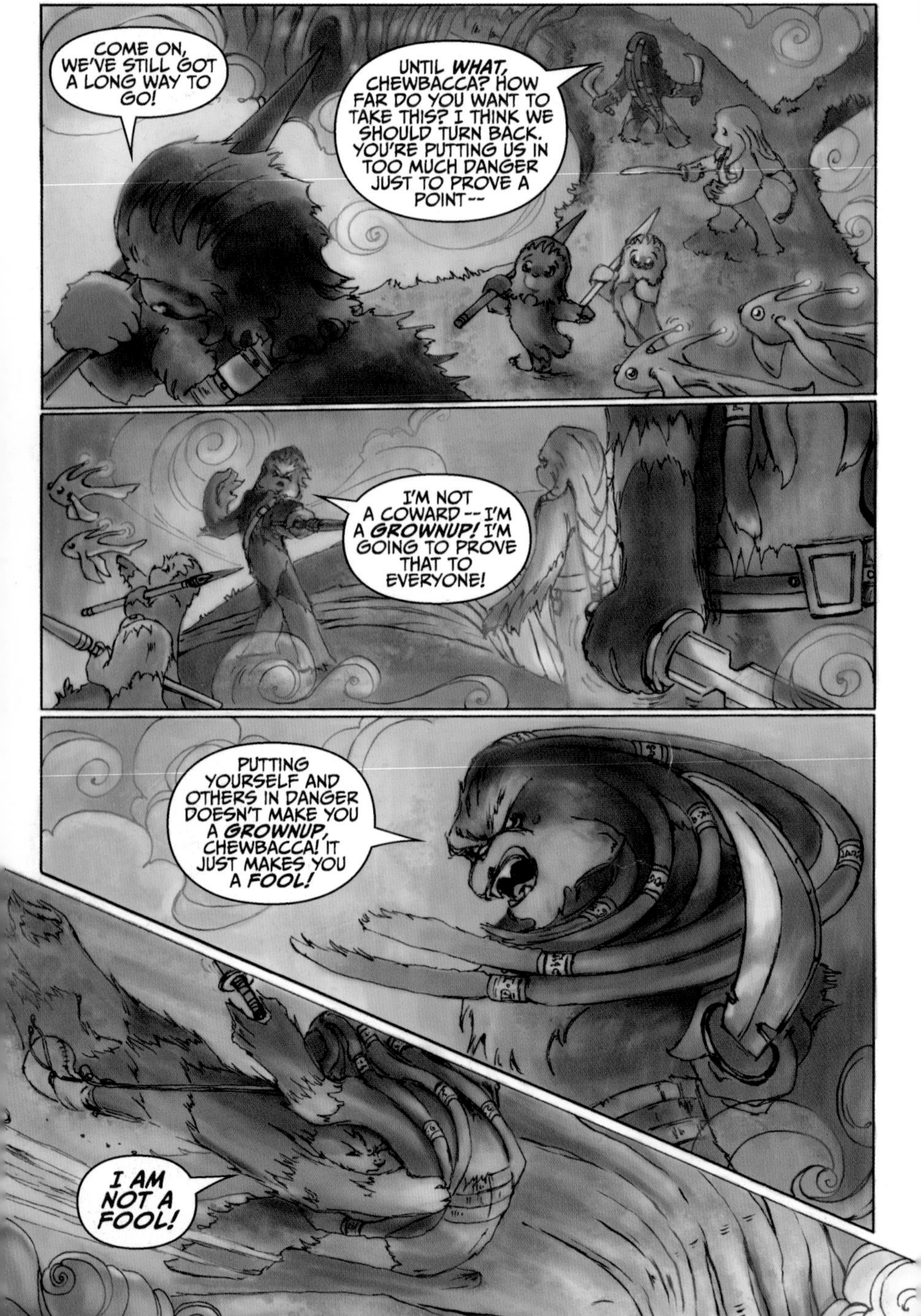
COME ON, WE'VE STILL GOT A LONG WAY TO GO!
UNTIL *WHAT*, CHEWBACCA? HOW FAR DO YOU WANT TO TAKE THIS? I THINK WE SHOULD TURN BACK. YOU'RE PUTTING US IN TOO MUCH DANGER JUST TO PROVE A POINT--
I'M NOT A COWARD--I'M A *GROWNUP!* I'M GOING TO PROVE THAT TO EVERYONE!
PUTTING YOURSELF AND OTHERS IN DANGER DOESN'T MAKE YOU A *GROWNUP*, CHEWBACCA! IT JUST MAKES YOU A *FOOL!*
I AM NOT A FOOL!

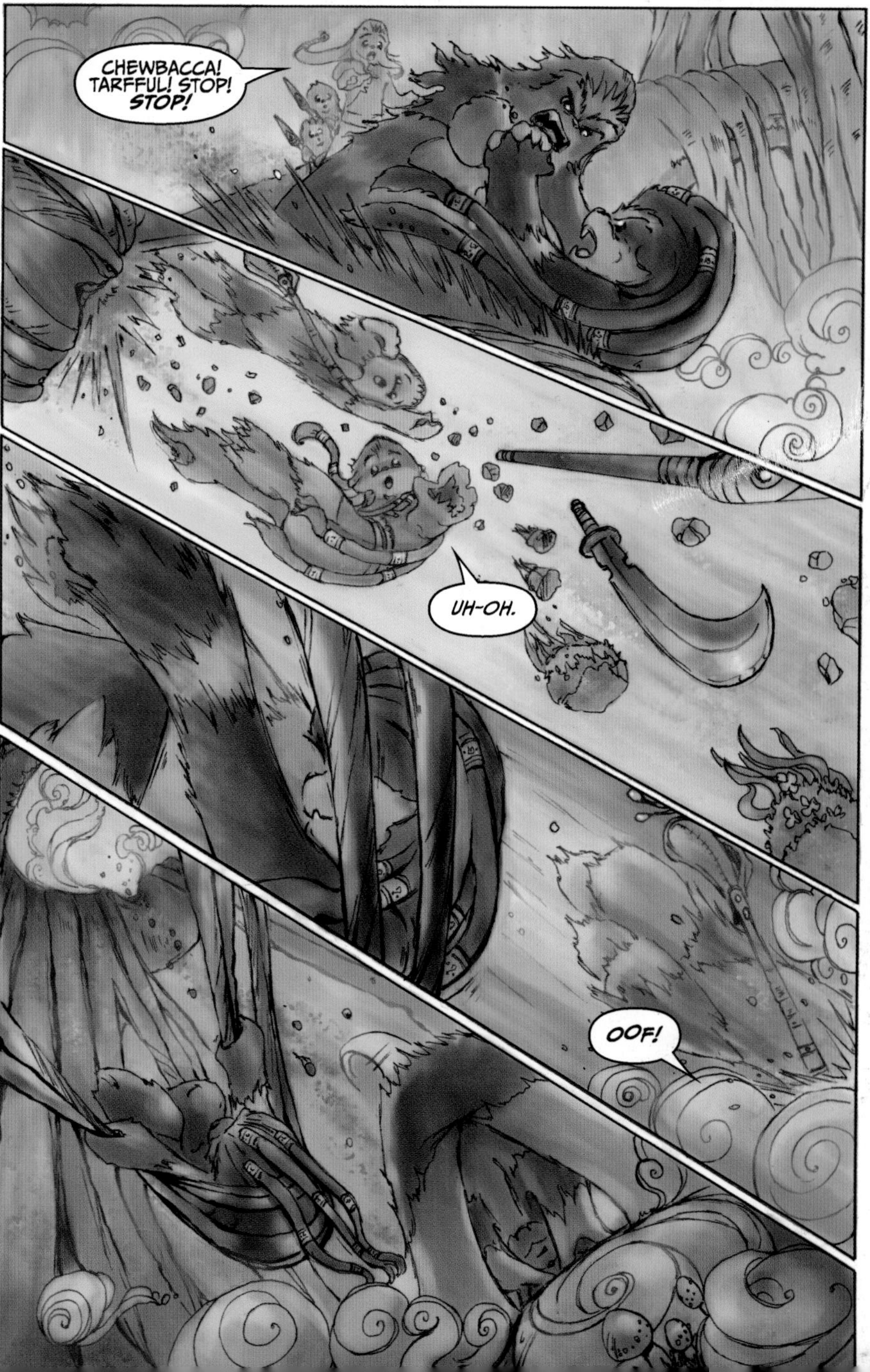
CHEWBACCA! TARFFUL! STOP! STOP!
UH-OH.
OOF!

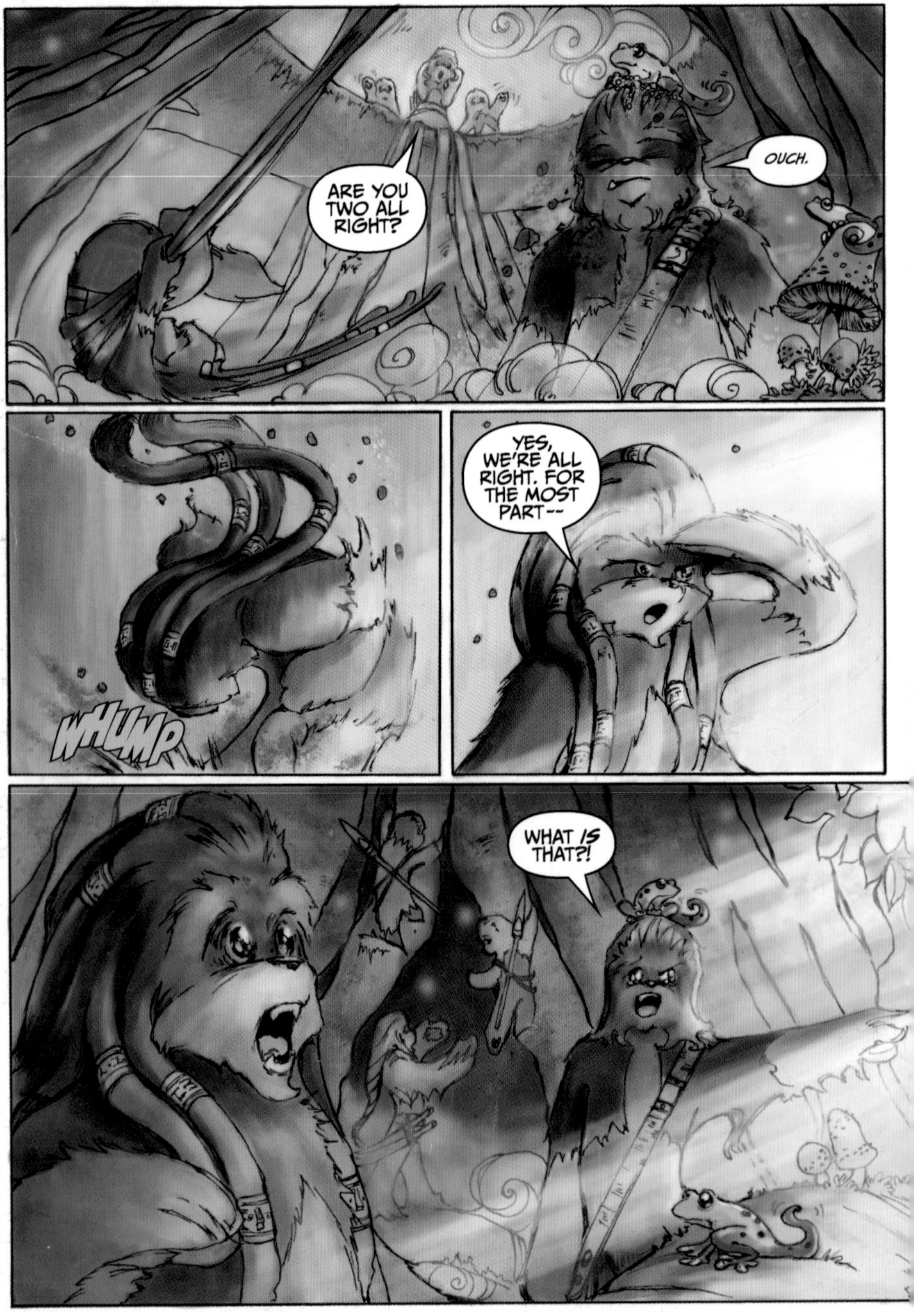
ARE YOU TWO ALL RIGHT?
OUCH.
WHUMP
YES, WE'RE ALL RIGHT. FOR THE MOST PART--
WHAT IS THAT?!

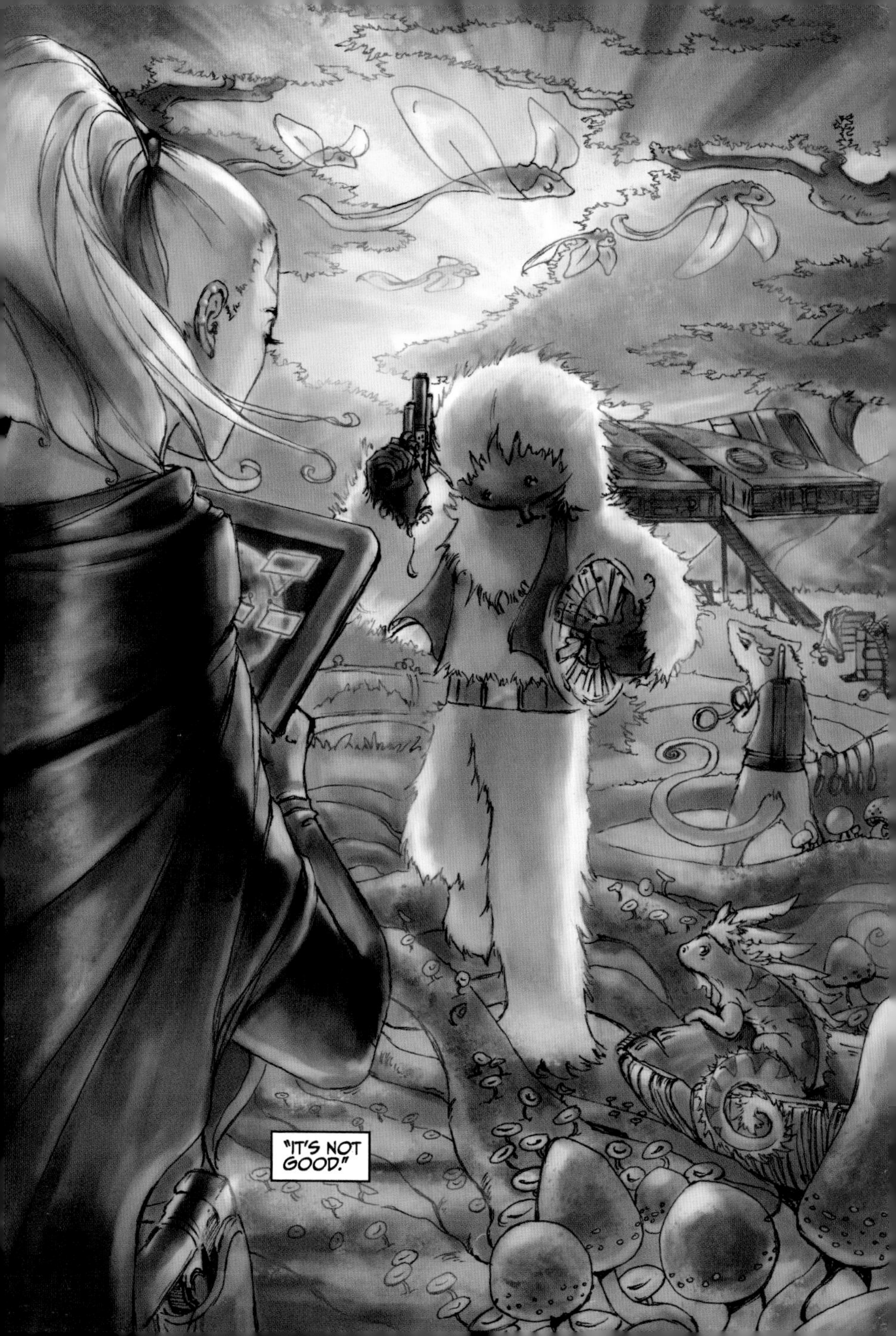
"IT'S NOT GOOD."

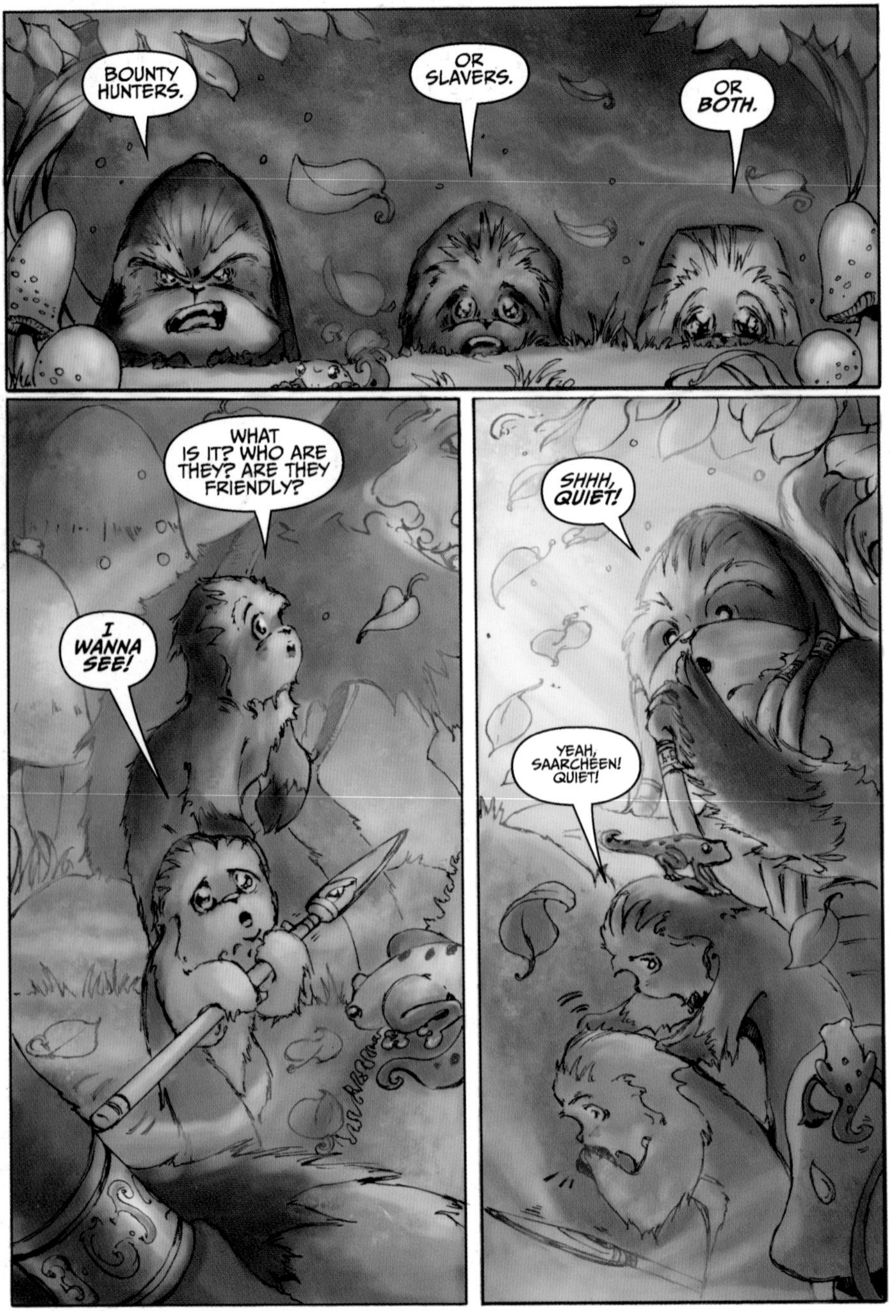

BOUNTY HUNTERS.
OR SLAVERS.
OR BOTH.
WHAT IS IT? WHO ARE THEY? ARE THEY FRIENDLY?
I WANNA SEE!
SHHH, QUIET!
YEAH, SAARCHEEN! QUIET!

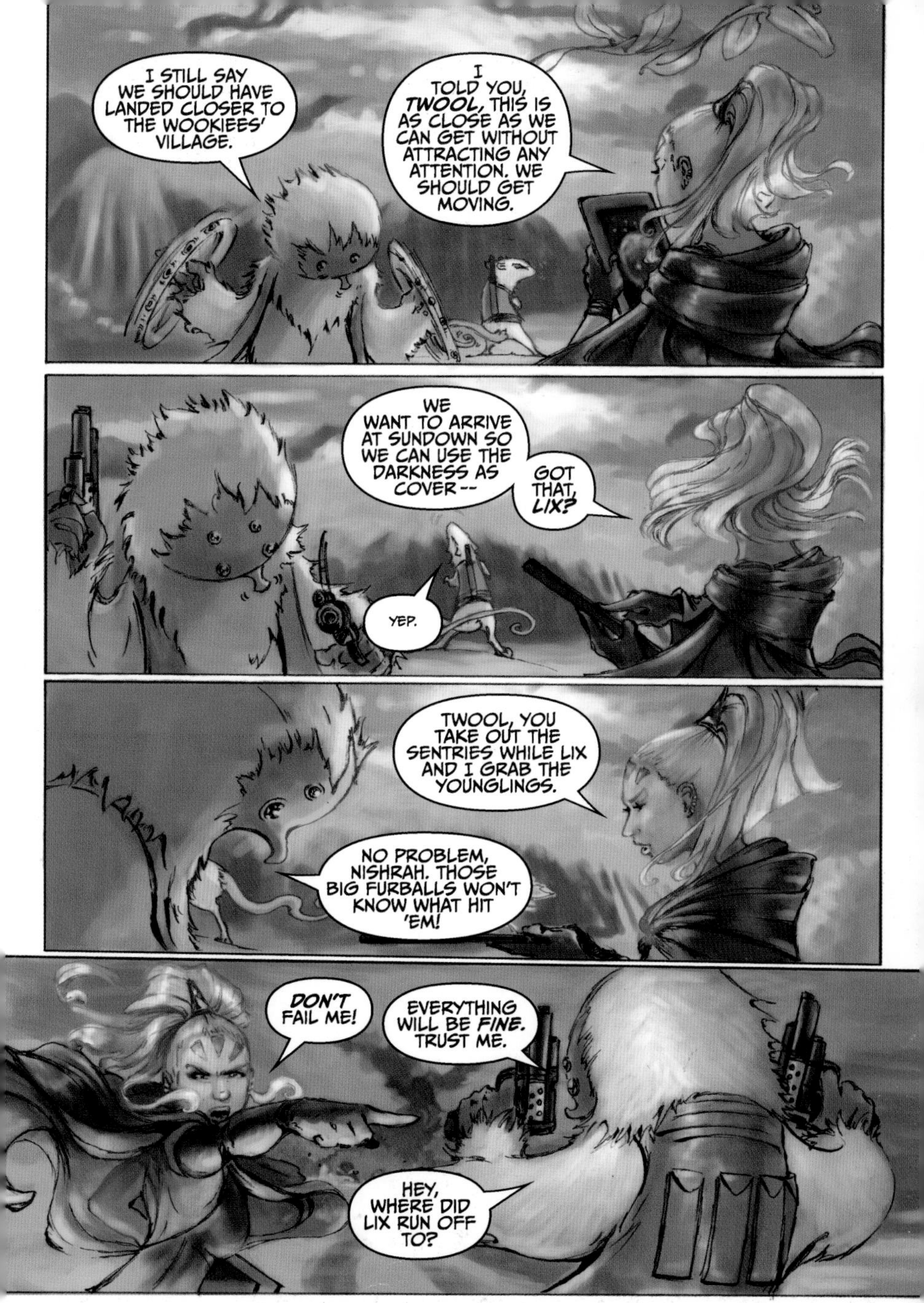
I STILL SAY WE SHOULD HAVE LANDED CLOSER TO THE WOOKIEES' VILLAGE.
I TOLD YOU, TWOOL, THIS IS AS CLOSE AS WE CAN GET WITHOUT ATTRACTING ANY ATTENTION. WE SHOULD GET MOVING.
WE WANT TO ARRIVE AT SUNDOWN SO WE CAN USE THE DARKNESS AS COVER--
GOT THAT, LIX?
YEP.
TWOOL, YOU TAKE OUT THE SENTRIES WHILE LIX AND I GRAB THE YOUNGLINGS.
NO PROBLEM, NISHRAH. THOSE BIG FURBALLS WON'T KNOW WHAT HIT 'EM!
DON'T FAIL ME!
EVERYTHING WILL BE FINE. TRUST ME.
HEY, WHERE DID LIX RUN OFF TO?

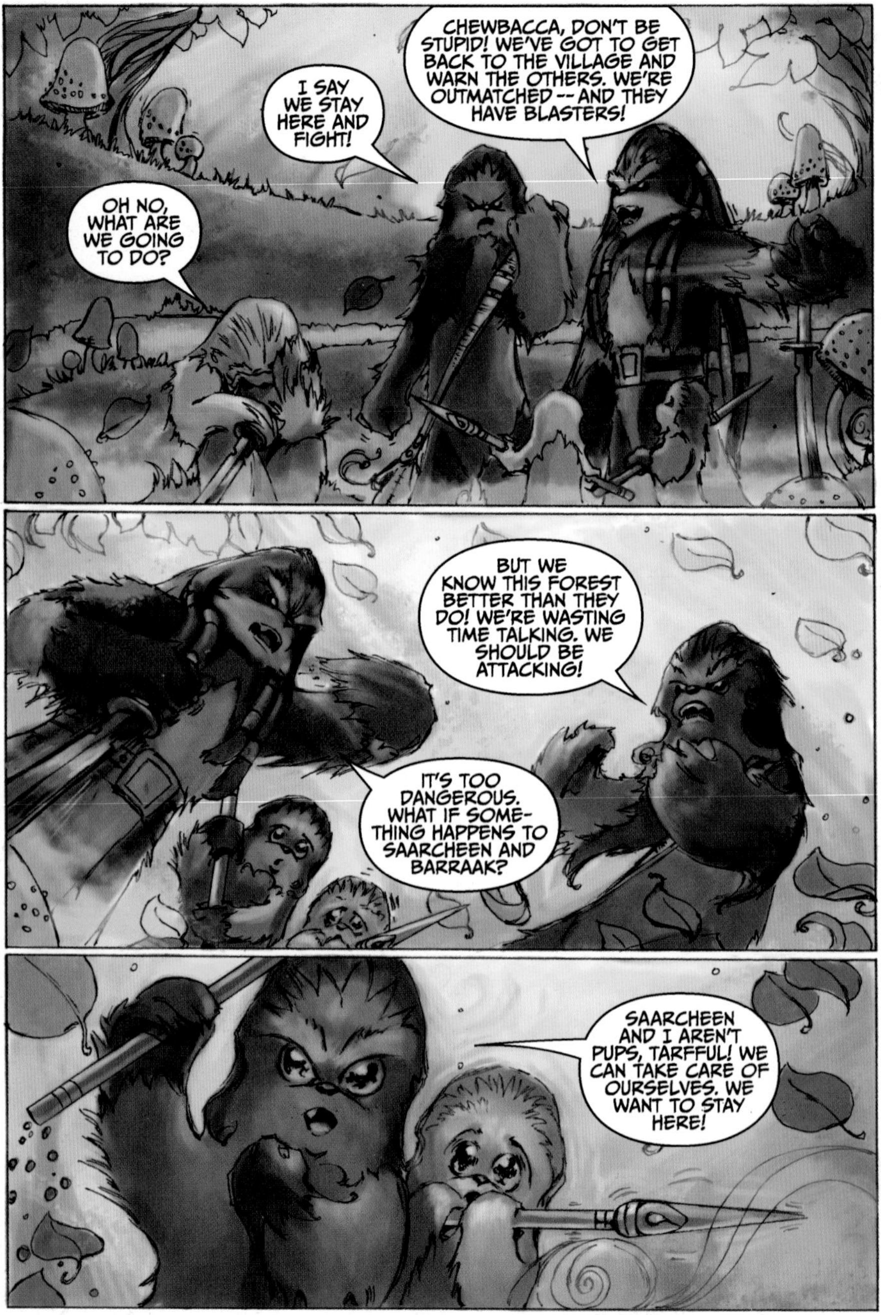
OH NO, WHAT ARE WE GOING TO DO?
I SAY WE STAY HERE AND FIGHT!
CHEWBACCA, DON'T BE STUPID! WE'VE GOT TO GET BACK TO THE VILLAGE AND WARN THE OTHERS. WE'RE OUTMATCHED -- AND THEY HAVE BLASTERS!
BUT WE KNOW THIS FOREST BETTER THAN THEY DO! WE'RE WASTING TIME TALKING. WE SHOULD BE ATTACKING!
IT'S TOO DANGEROUS. WHAT IF SOMETHING HAPPENS TO SAARCHEEN AND BARRAAK?
SAARCHEEN AND I AREN'T PUPS, TARFFUL! WE CAN TAKE CARE OF OURSELVES. WE WANT TO STAY HERE!

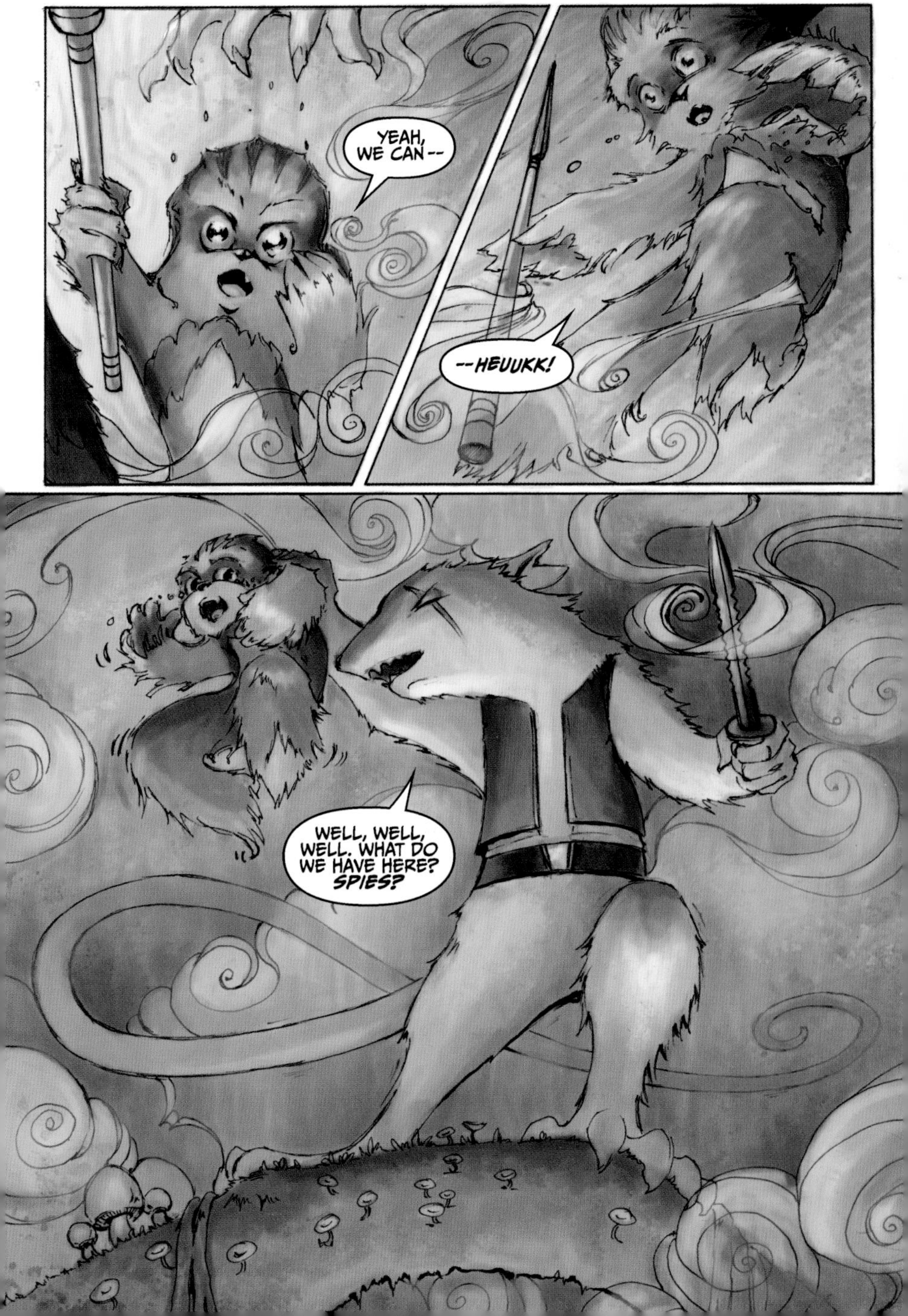
YEAH, WE CAN--
--HEUUKK!
WELL, WELL, WELL. WHAT DO WE HAVE HERE? SPIES?

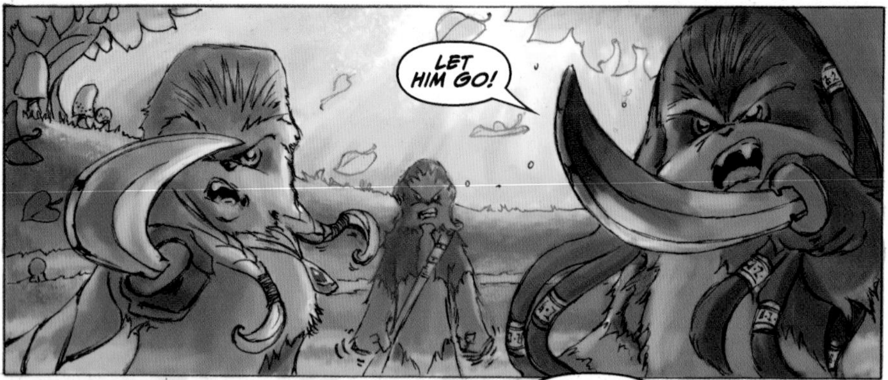
LET HIM GO!

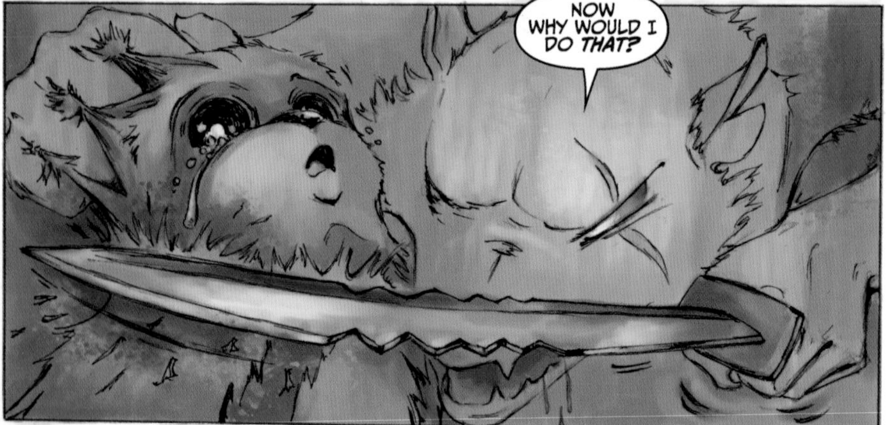
NOW WHY WOULD I DO *THAT?*

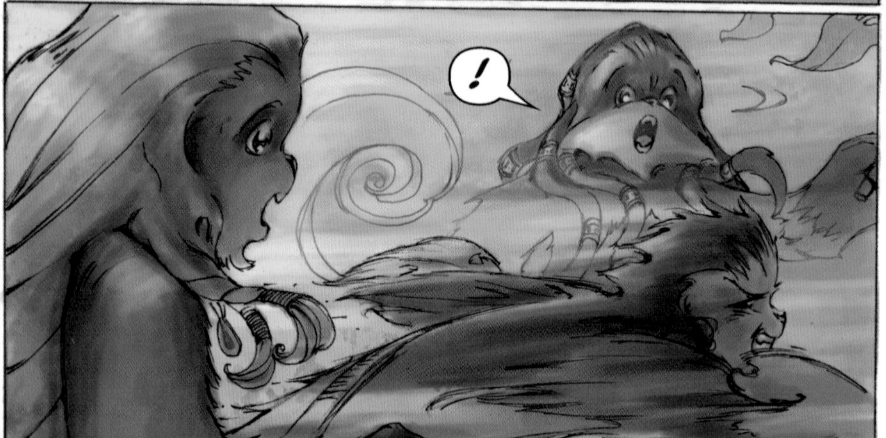
!

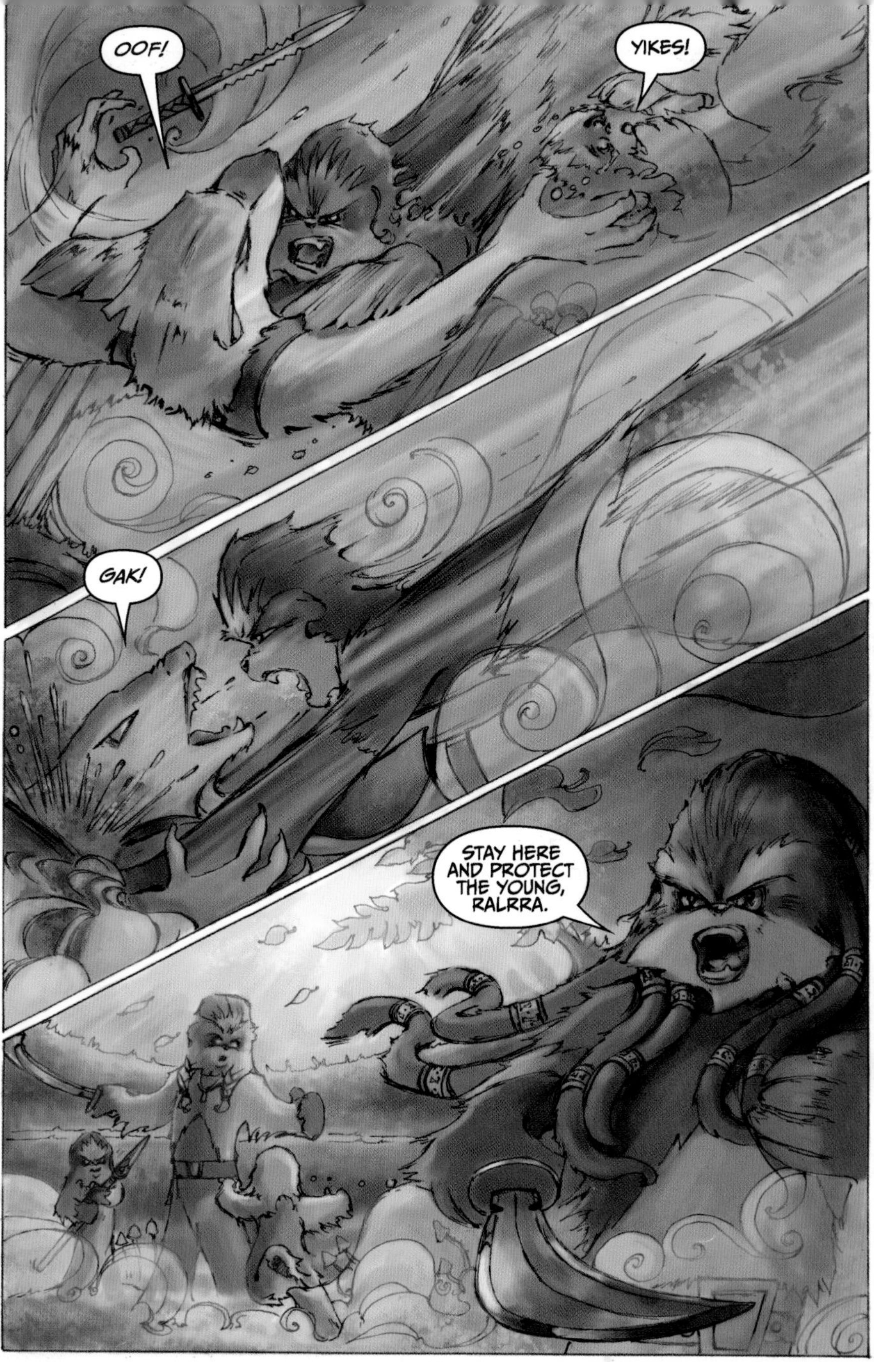
OOF!
YIKES!
GAK!
STAY HERE AND PROTECT THE YOUNG, RALRRA.

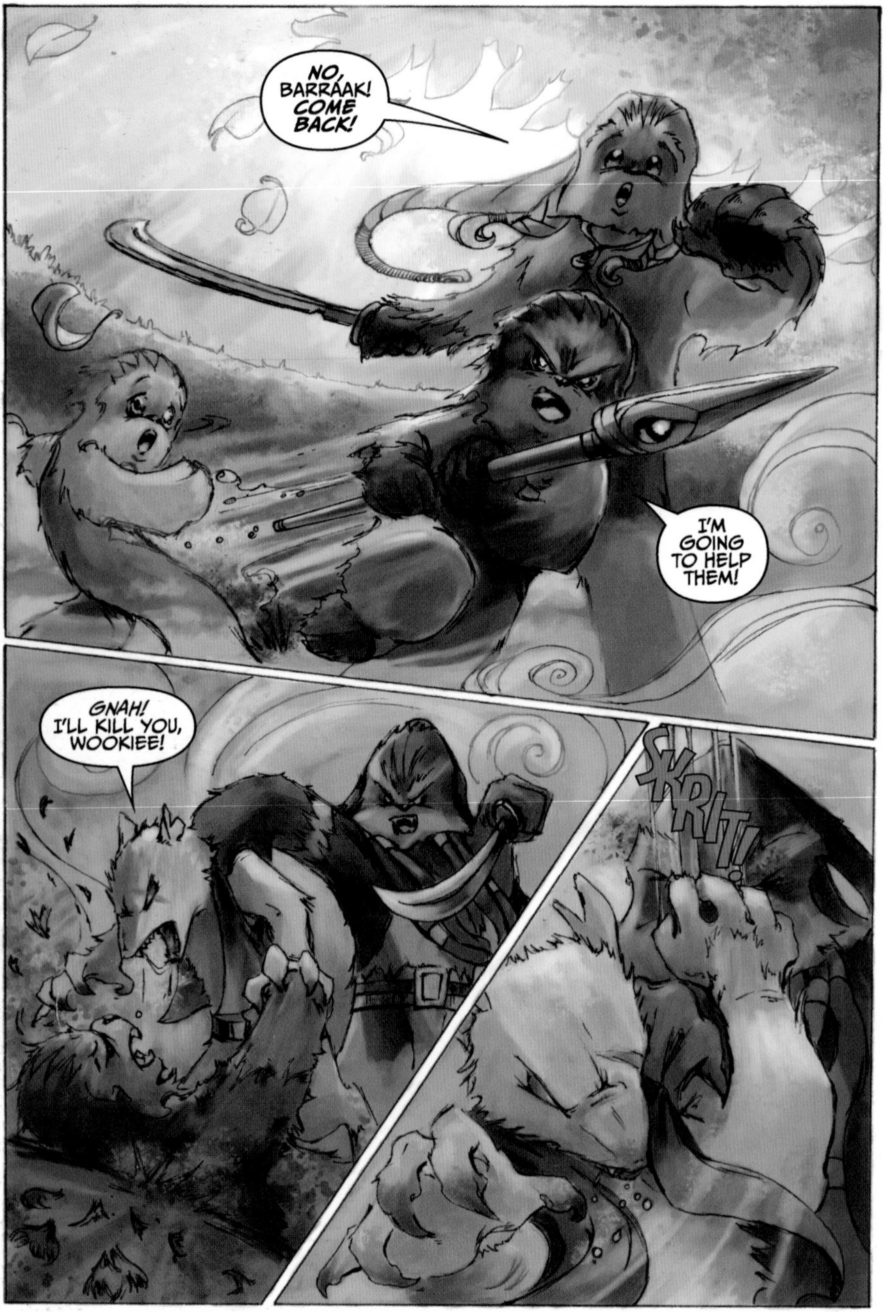
NO, BARRAAK! COME BACK!
I'M GOING TO HELP THEM!
GNAH! I'LL KILL YOU, WOOKIEE!
SKRIT!

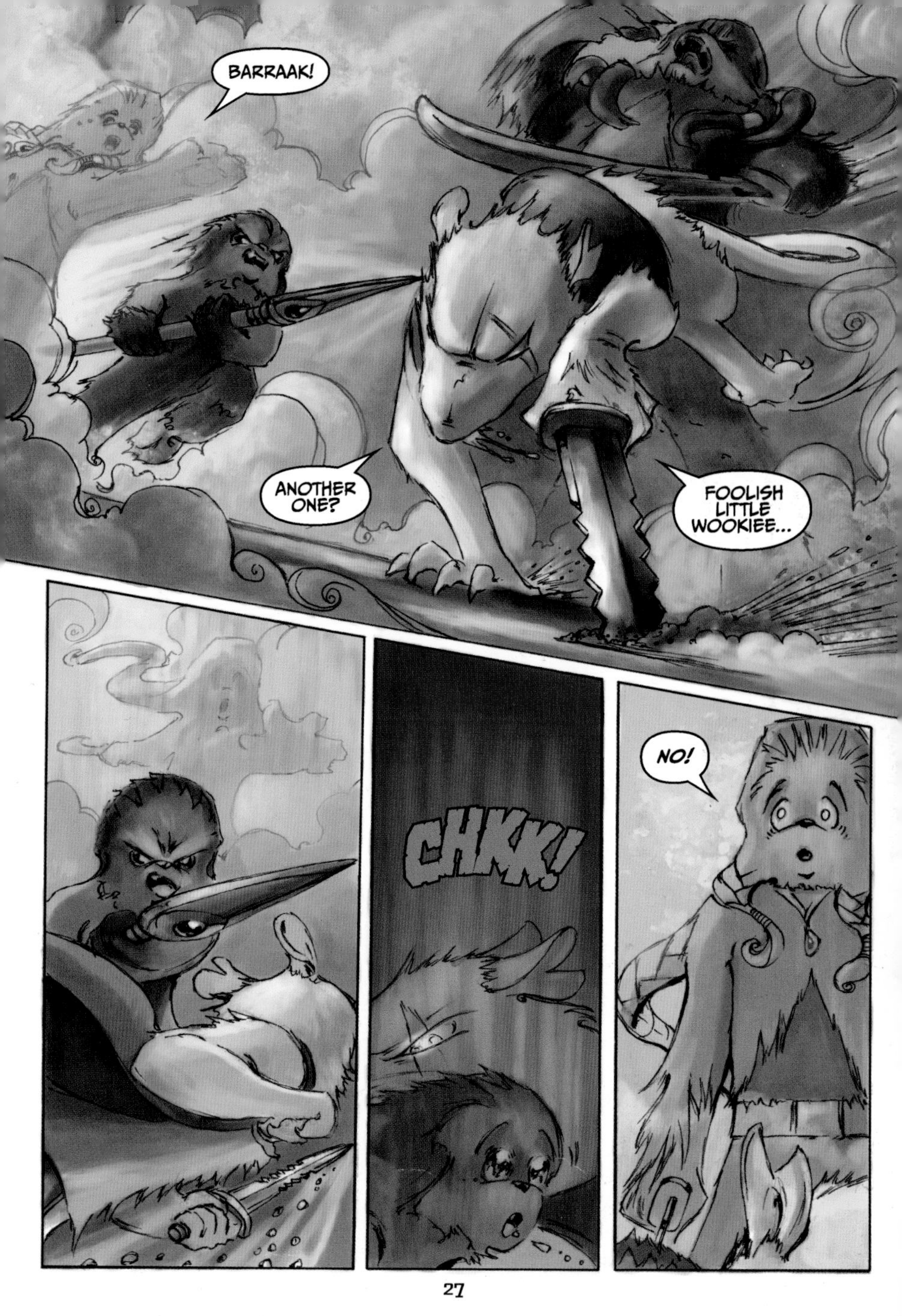
BARRAAK!
ANOTHER ONE?
FOOLISH LITTLE WOOKIEE...
CHKK!
NO!

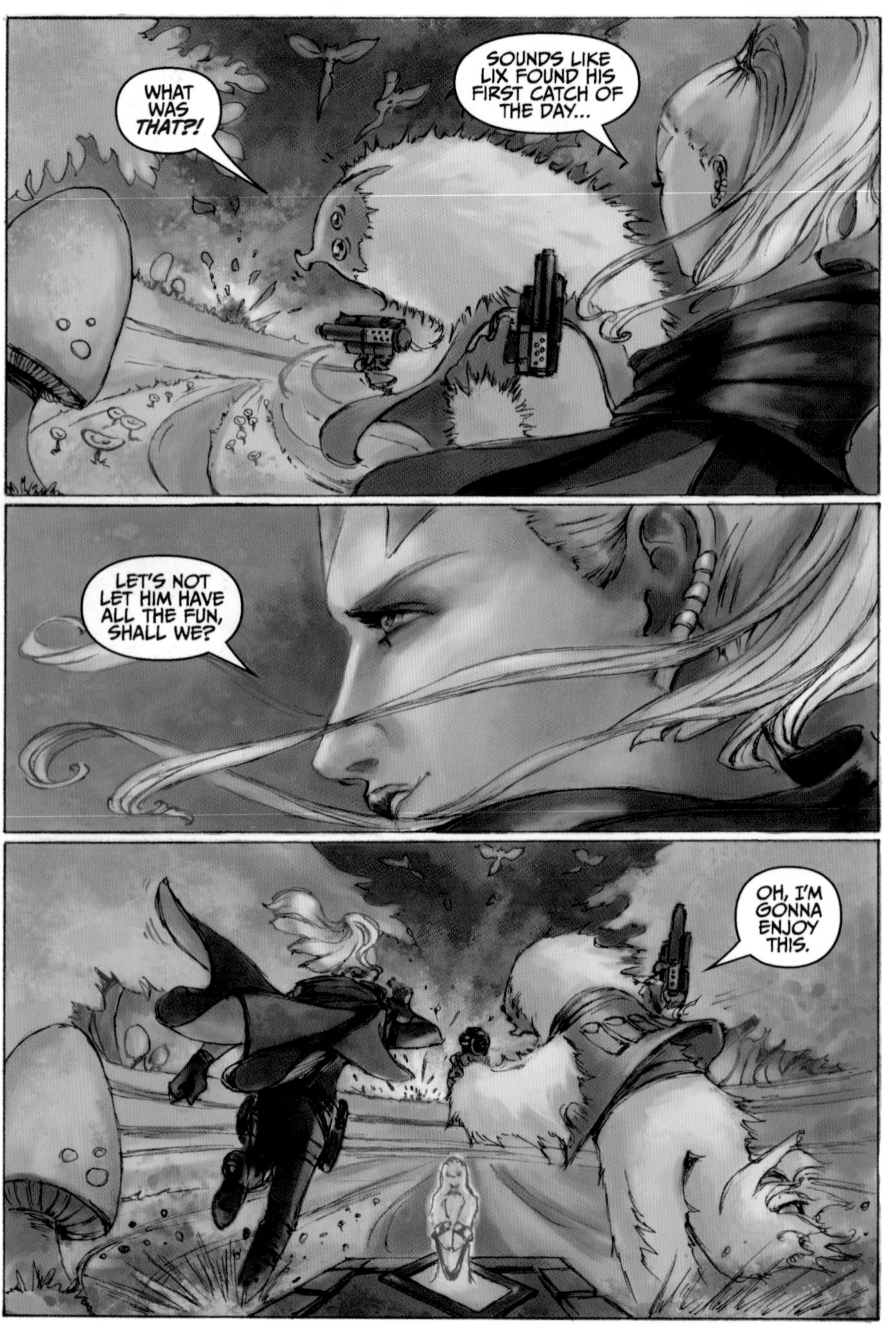
WHAT WAS THAT?!
SOUNDS LIKE LIX FOUND HIS FIRST CATCH OF THE DAY...
LET'S NOT LET HIM HAVE ALL THE FUN, SHALL WE?
OH, I'M GONNA ENJOY THIS.

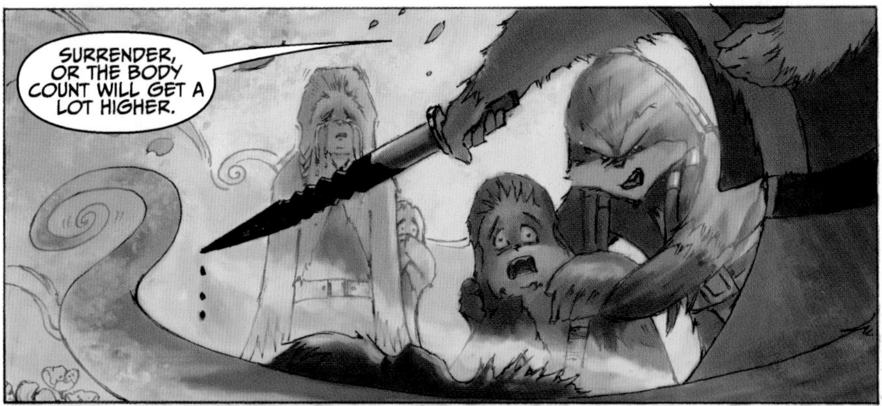
SURRENDER, OR THE BODY COUNT WILL GET A LOT HIGHER.

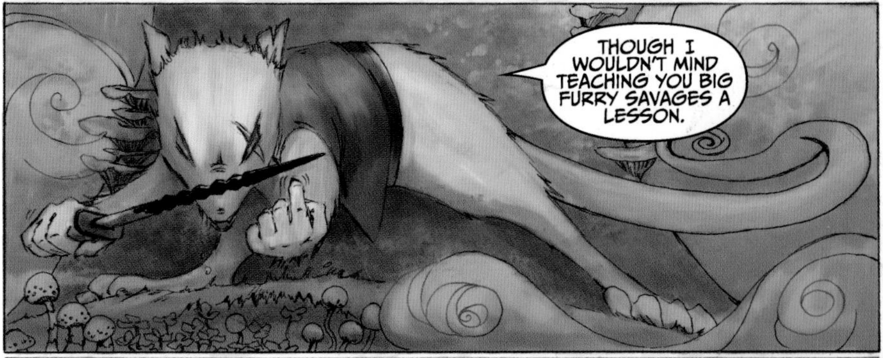
THOUGH I WOULDN'T MIND TEACHING YOU BIG FURRY SAVAGES A LESSON.

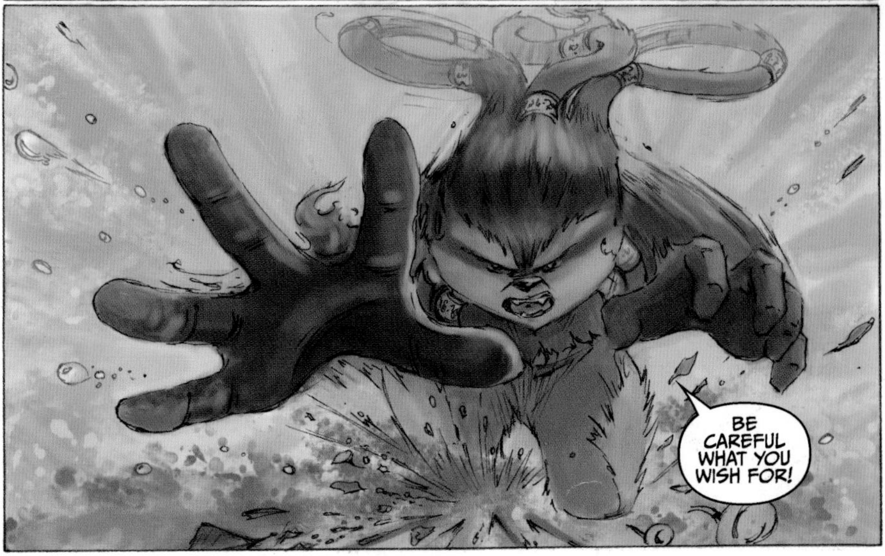
BE CAREFUL WHAT YOU WISH FOR!

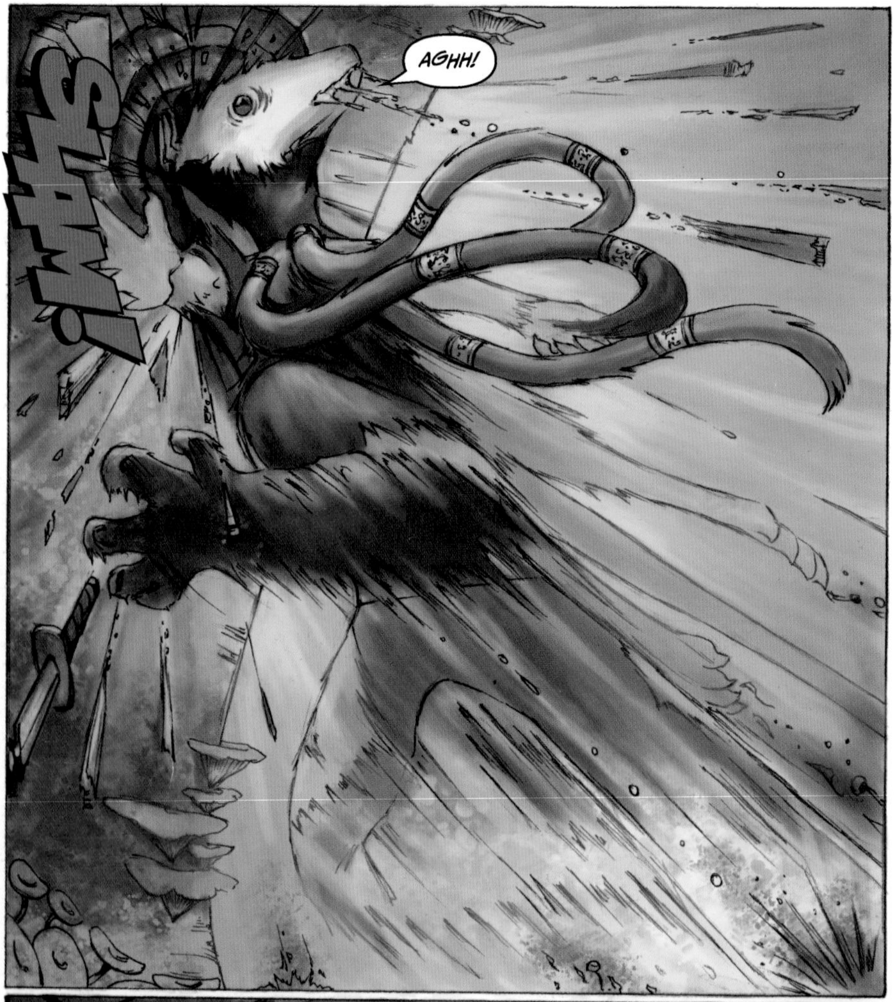
¡SHAW!
AGHH!

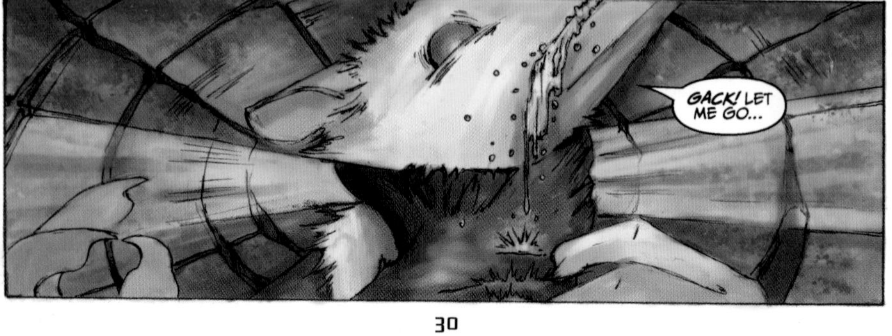
GACK! LET ME GO...

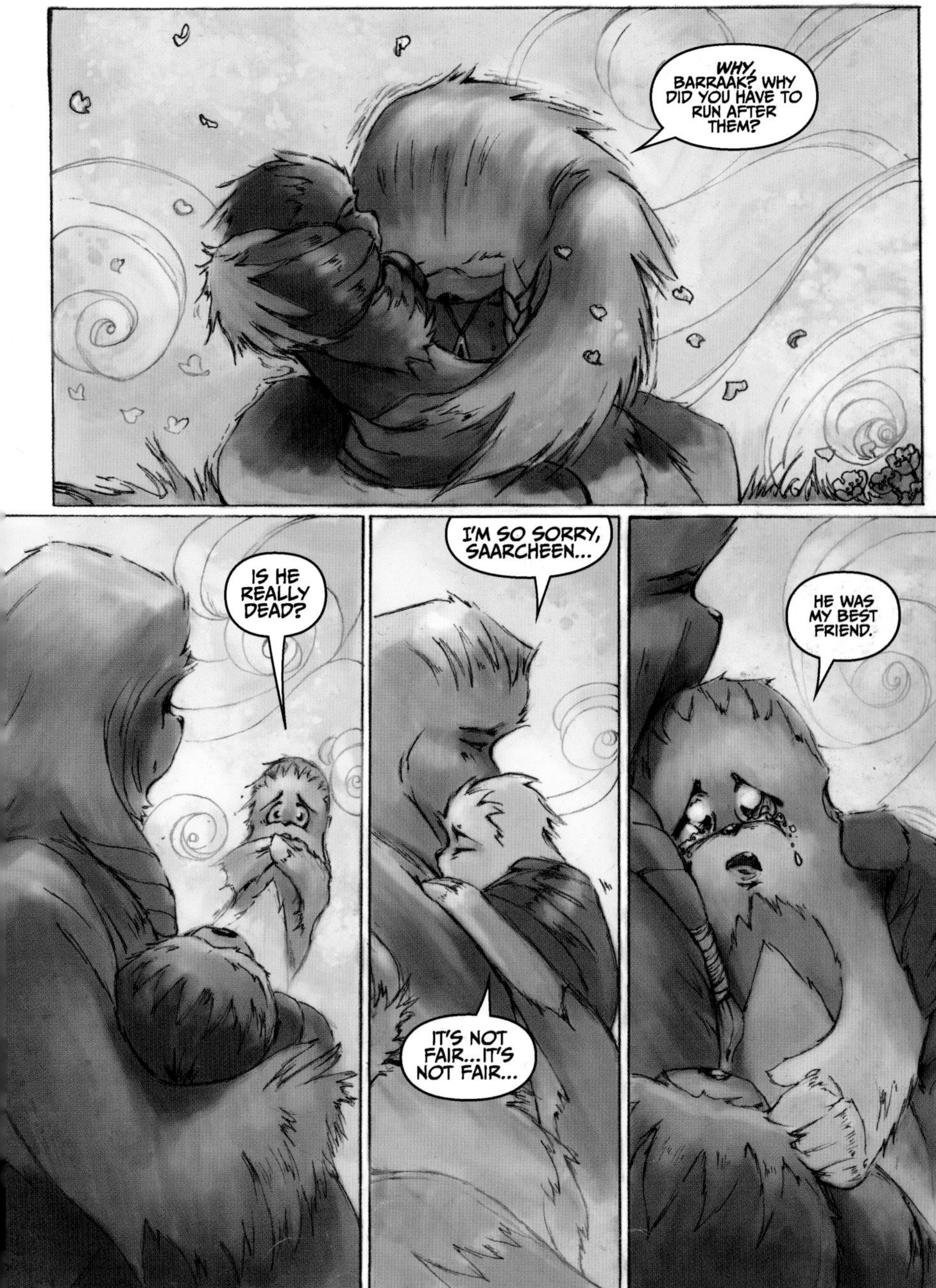
WHY, BARRAAK? WHY DID YOU HAVE TO RUN AFTER THEM?
IS HE REALLY DEAD?
I'M SO SORRY, SAARCHEEN...
IT'S NOT FAIR...IT'S NOT FAIR...
HE WAS MY BEST FRIEND.

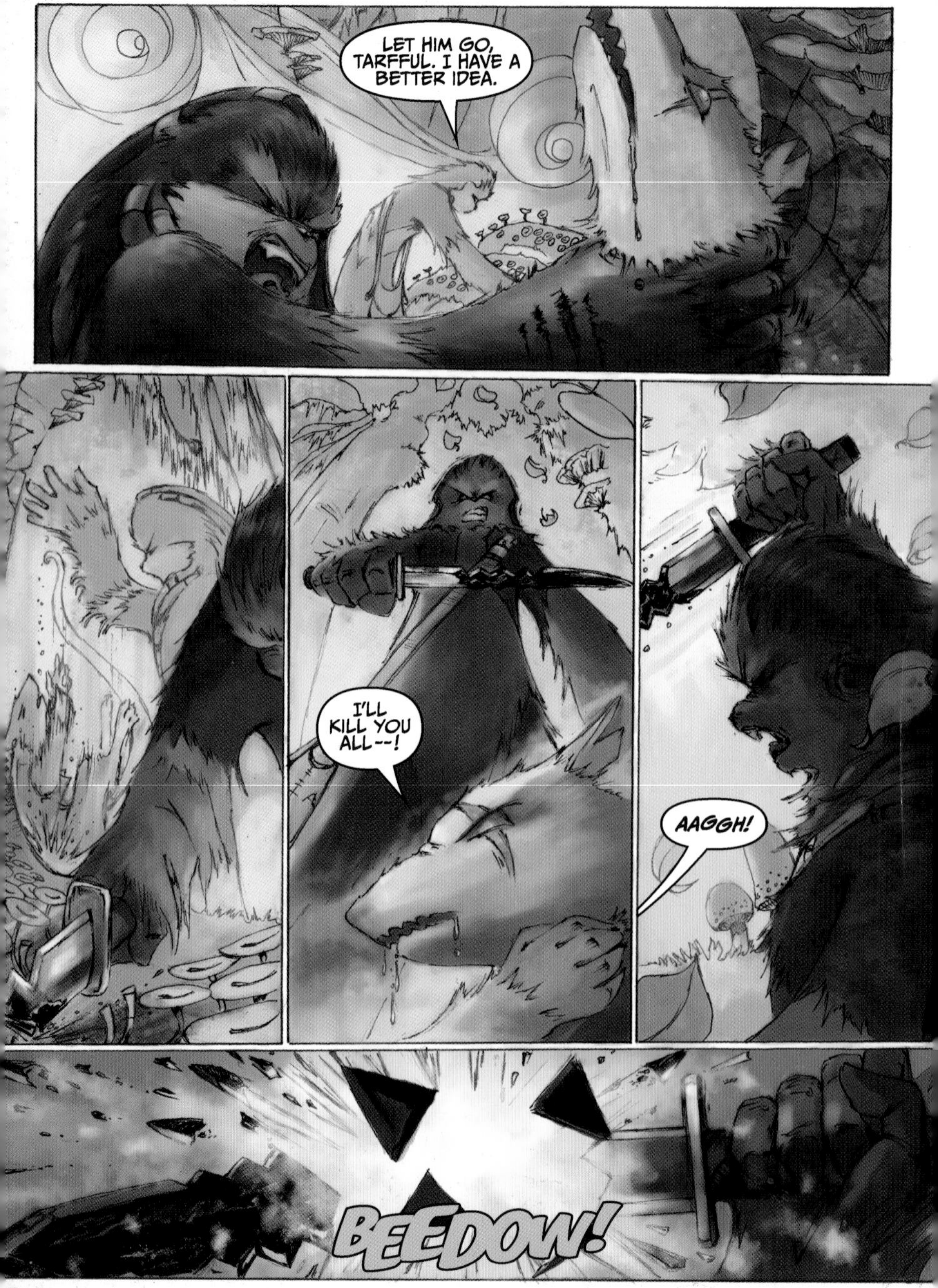
LET HIM GO, TARFFUL. I HAVE A BETTER IDEA.
I'LL KILL YOU ALL--!
AAGGH!
BEEDOW!

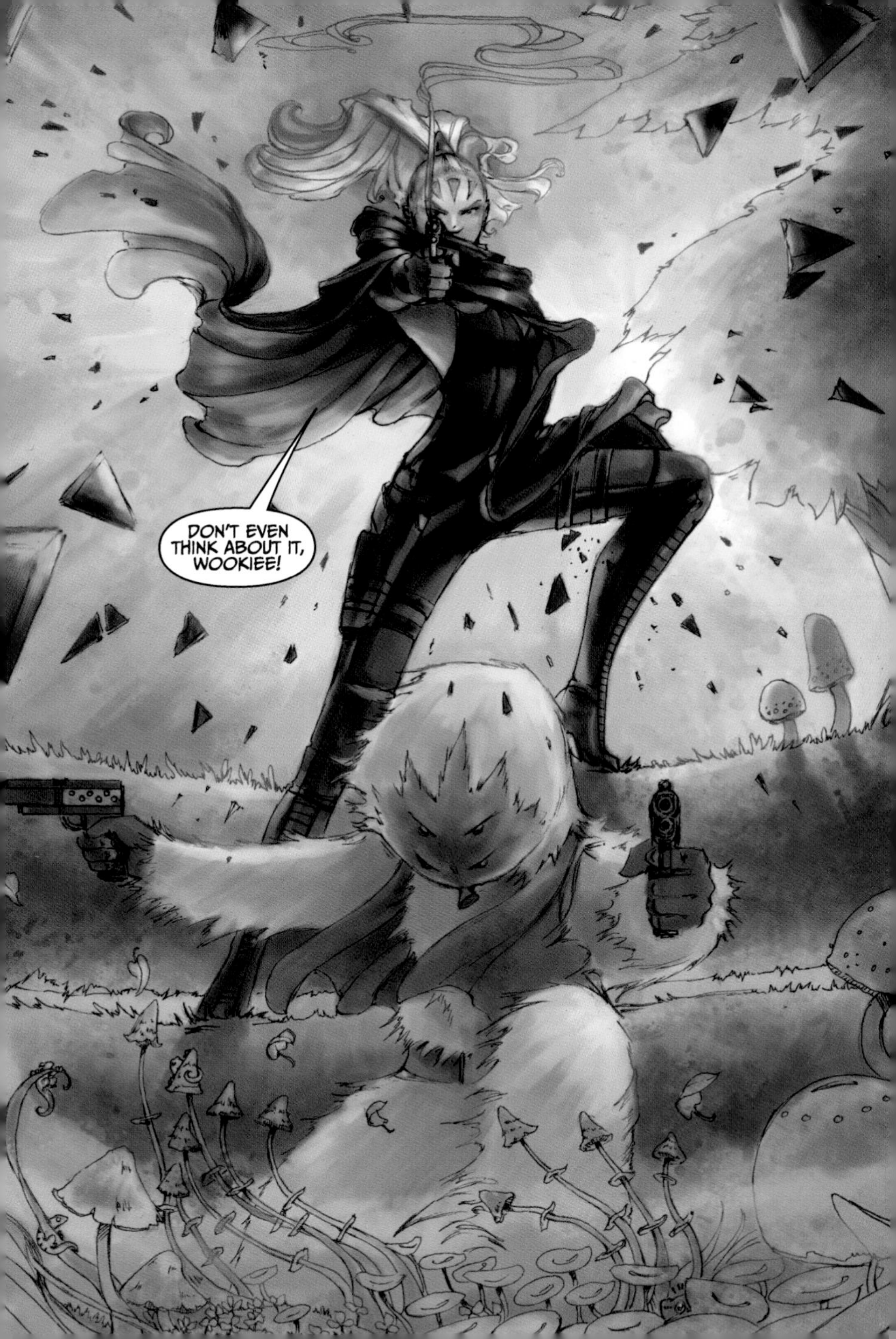
DON'T EVEN THINK ABOUT IT, WOOKIEE!

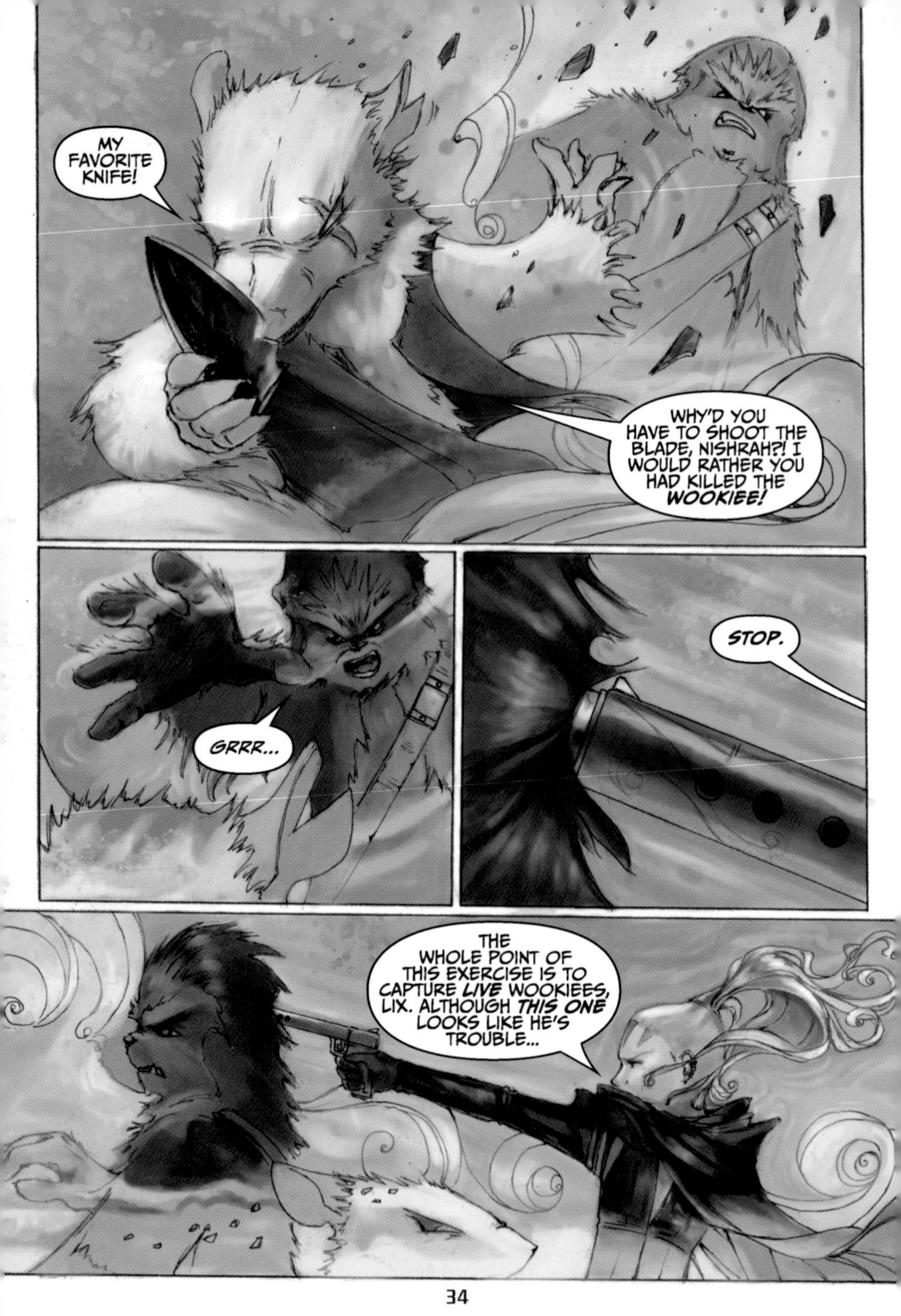
MY FAVORITE KNIFE!
WHY'D YOU HAVE TO SHOOT THE BLADE, NISHRAH?! I WOULD RATHER YOU HAD KILLED THE *WOOKIEE!*
GRRR...
STOP.
THE WHOLE POINT OF THIS EXERCISE IS TO CAPTURE *LIVE* WOOKIEES, LIX. ALTHOUGH *THIS ONE* LOOKS LIKE HE'S TROUBLE...

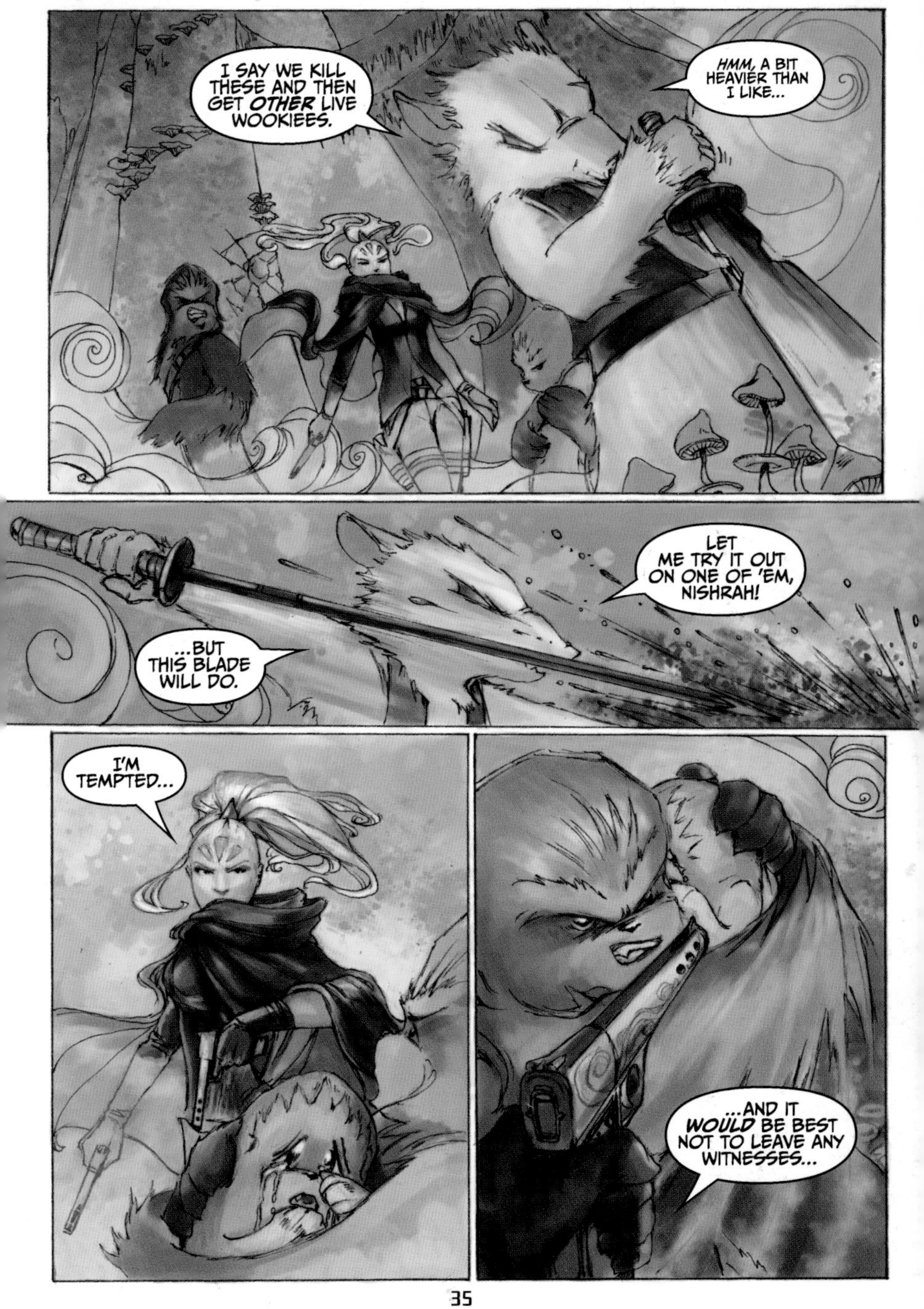

I SAY WE KILL THESE AND THEN GET *OTHER* LIVE WOOKIEES.
HMM, A BIT HEAVIER THAN I LIKE...
LET ME TRY IT OUT ON ONE OF 'EM, NISHRAH!
...BUT THIS BLADE WILL DO.
I'M TEMPTED...
...AND IT *WOULD* BE BEST NOT TO LEAVE ANY WITNESSES...

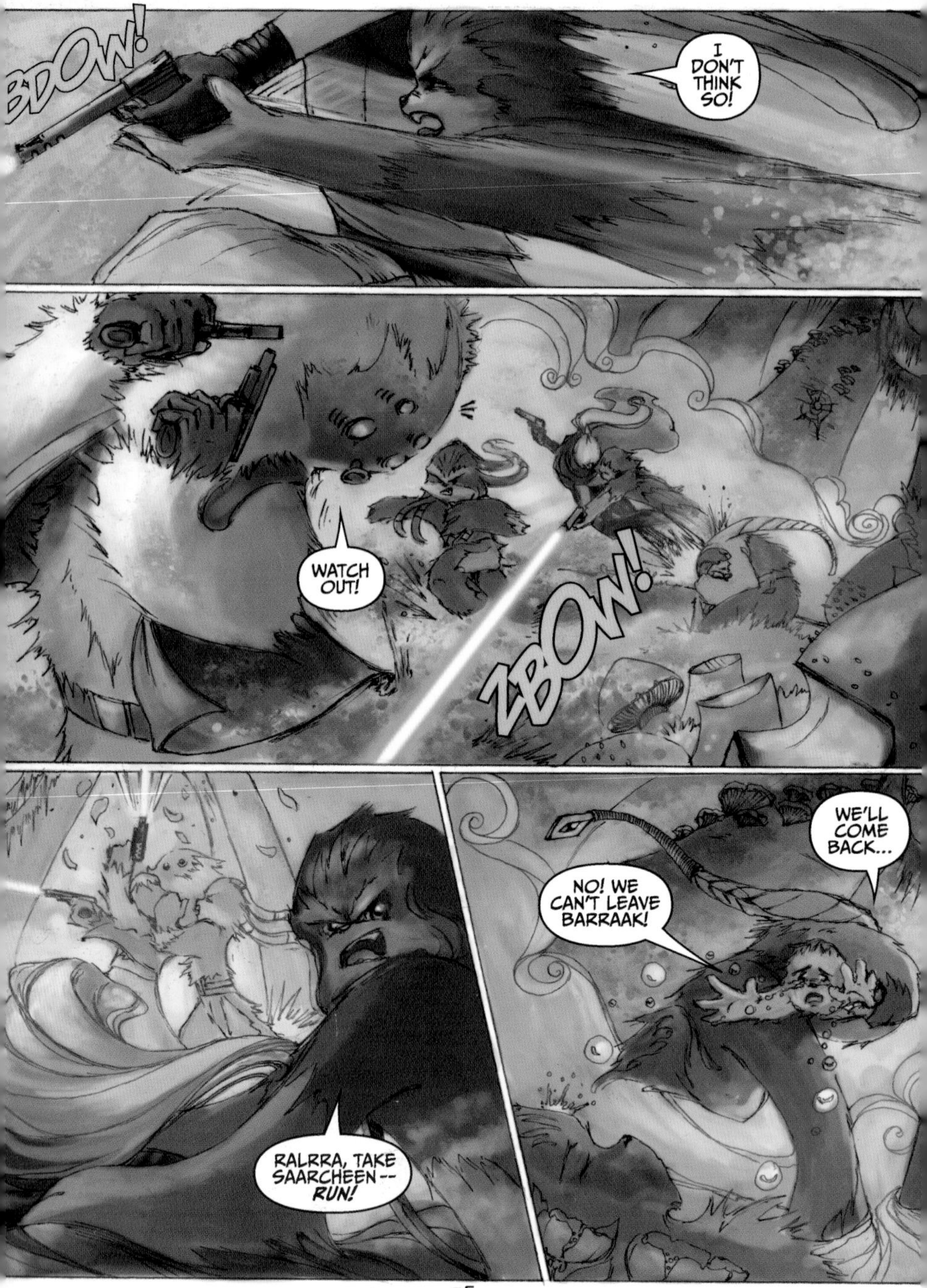
BDOW!
I DON'T THINK SO!
WATCH OUT!
ZBOW!
RALRRA, TAKE SAARCHEEN -- RUN!
NO! WE CAN'T LEAVE BARRAAK!
WE'LL COME BACK...

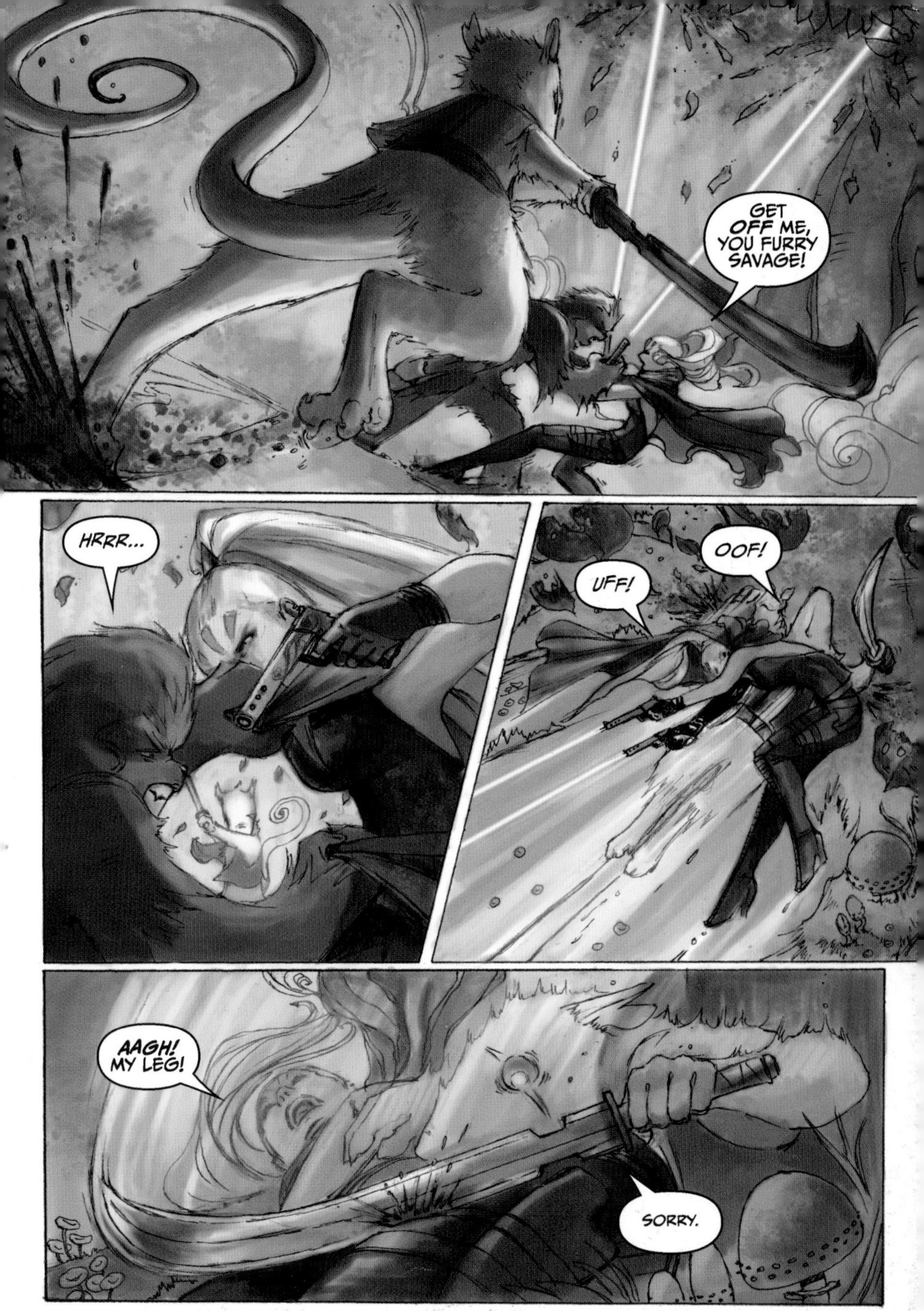
GET OFF ME, YOU FURRY SAVAGE!
HRRR...
UFF!
OOF!
AAGH! MY LEG!
SORRY.

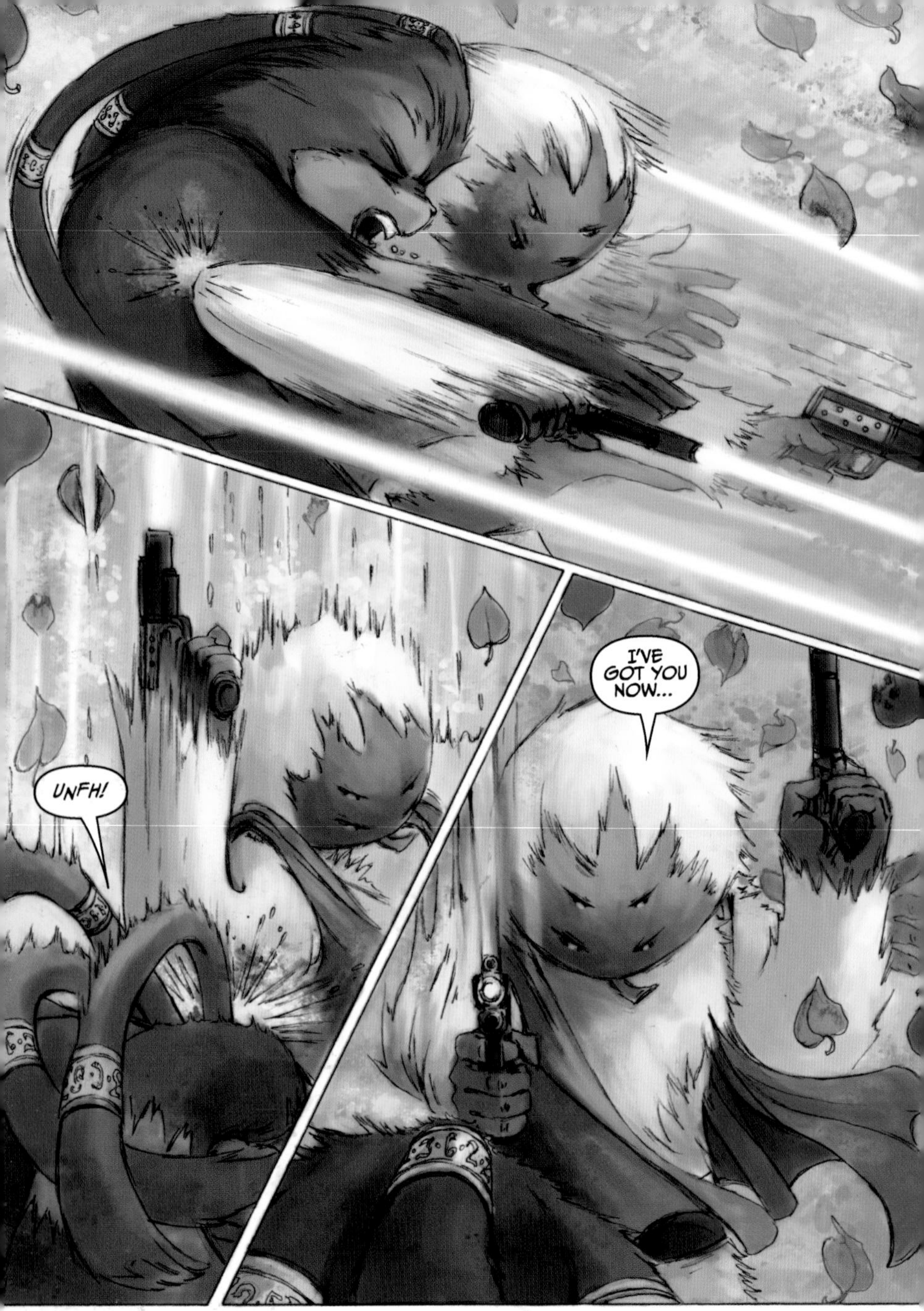
UNFH!
I'VE GOT YOU NOW...

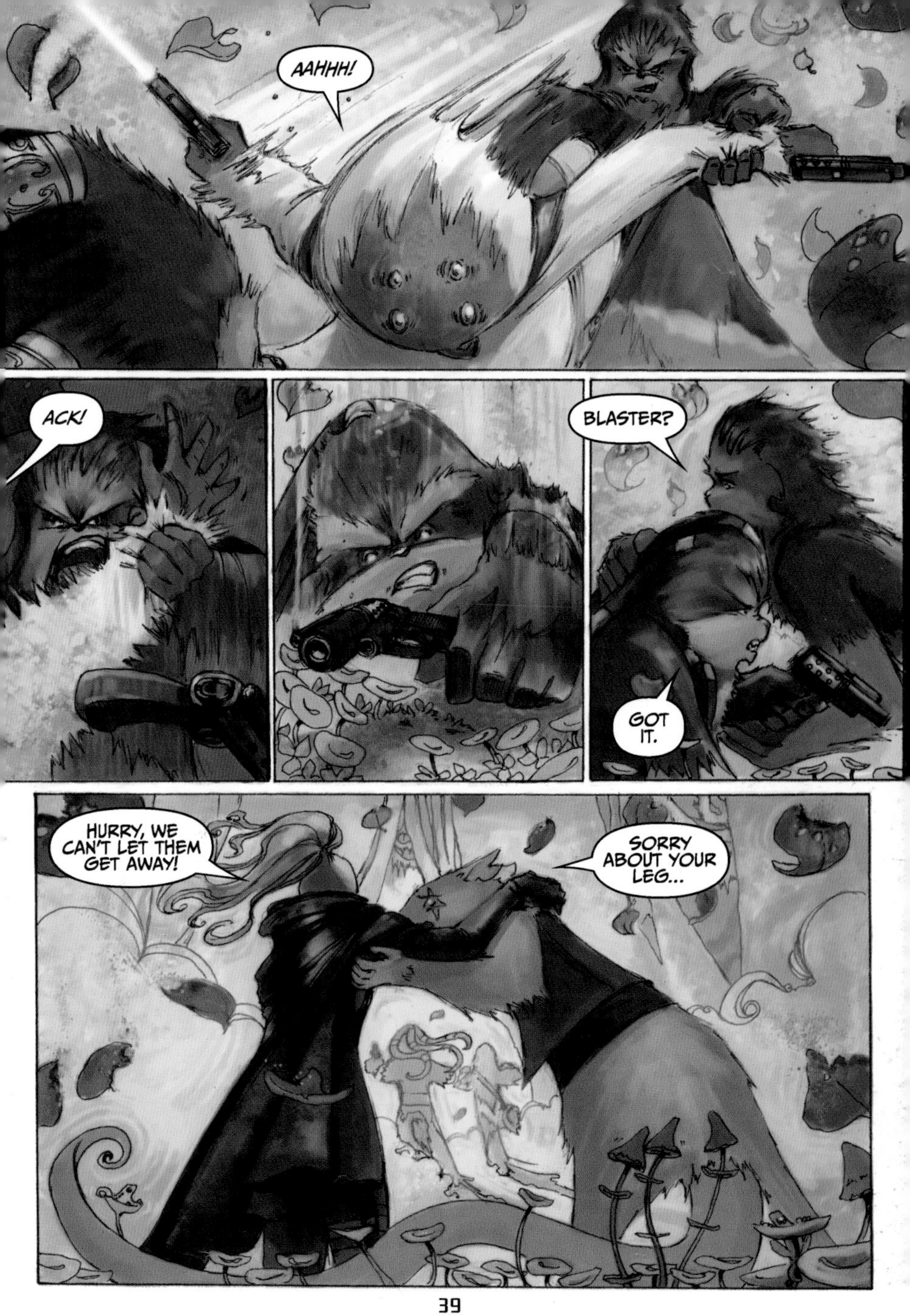
AAHHH!
ACK!
BLASTER?
GOT IT.
HURRY, WE CAN'T LET THEM GET AWAY!
SORRY ABOUT YOUR LEG...

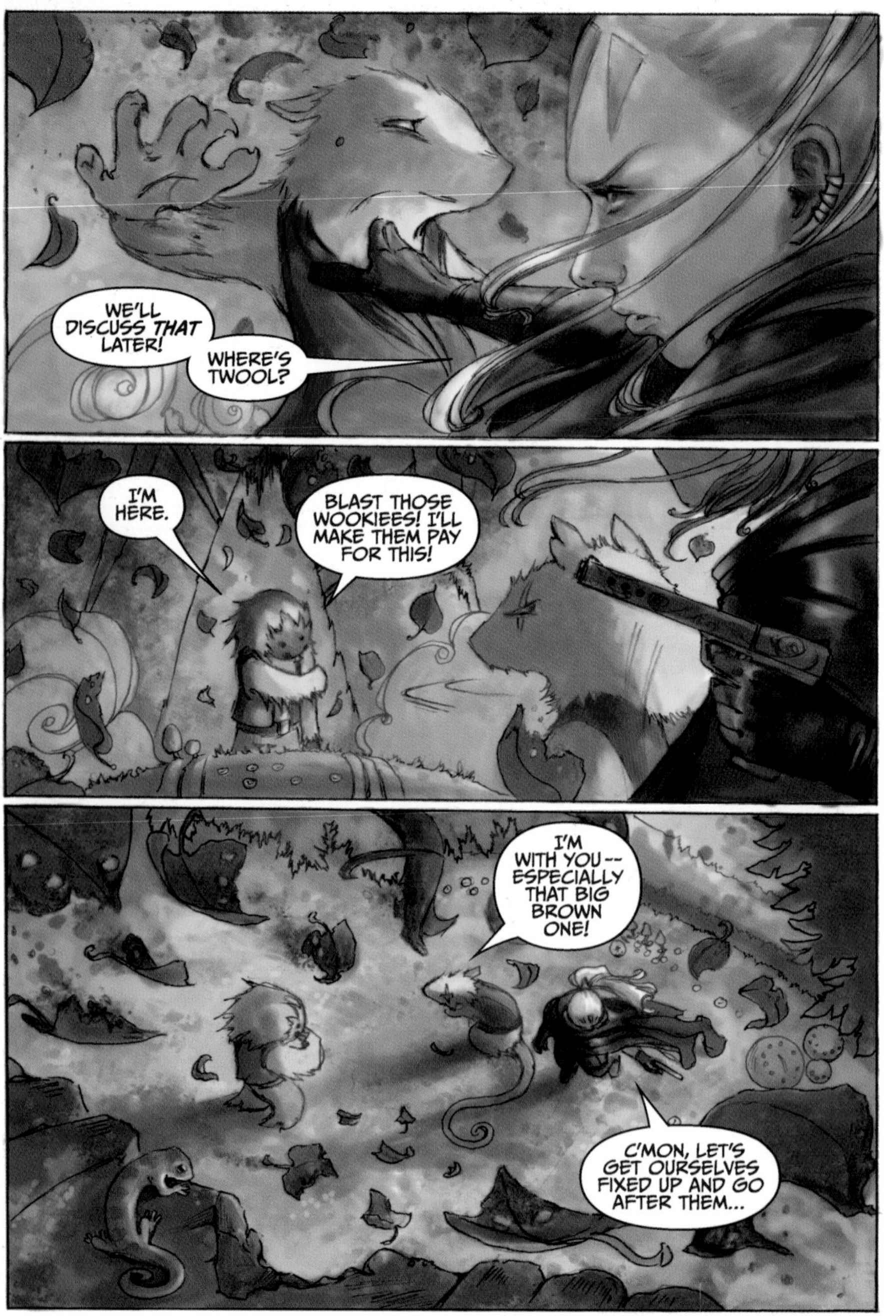

WE'LL DISCUSS THAT LATER!
WHERE'S TWOOL?
I'M HERE.
BLAST THOSE WOOKIEES! I'LL MAKE THEM PAY FOR THIS!
I'M WITH YOU -- ESPECIALLY THAT BIG BROWN ONE!
C'MON, LET'S GET OURSELVES FIXED UP AND GO AFTER THEM...

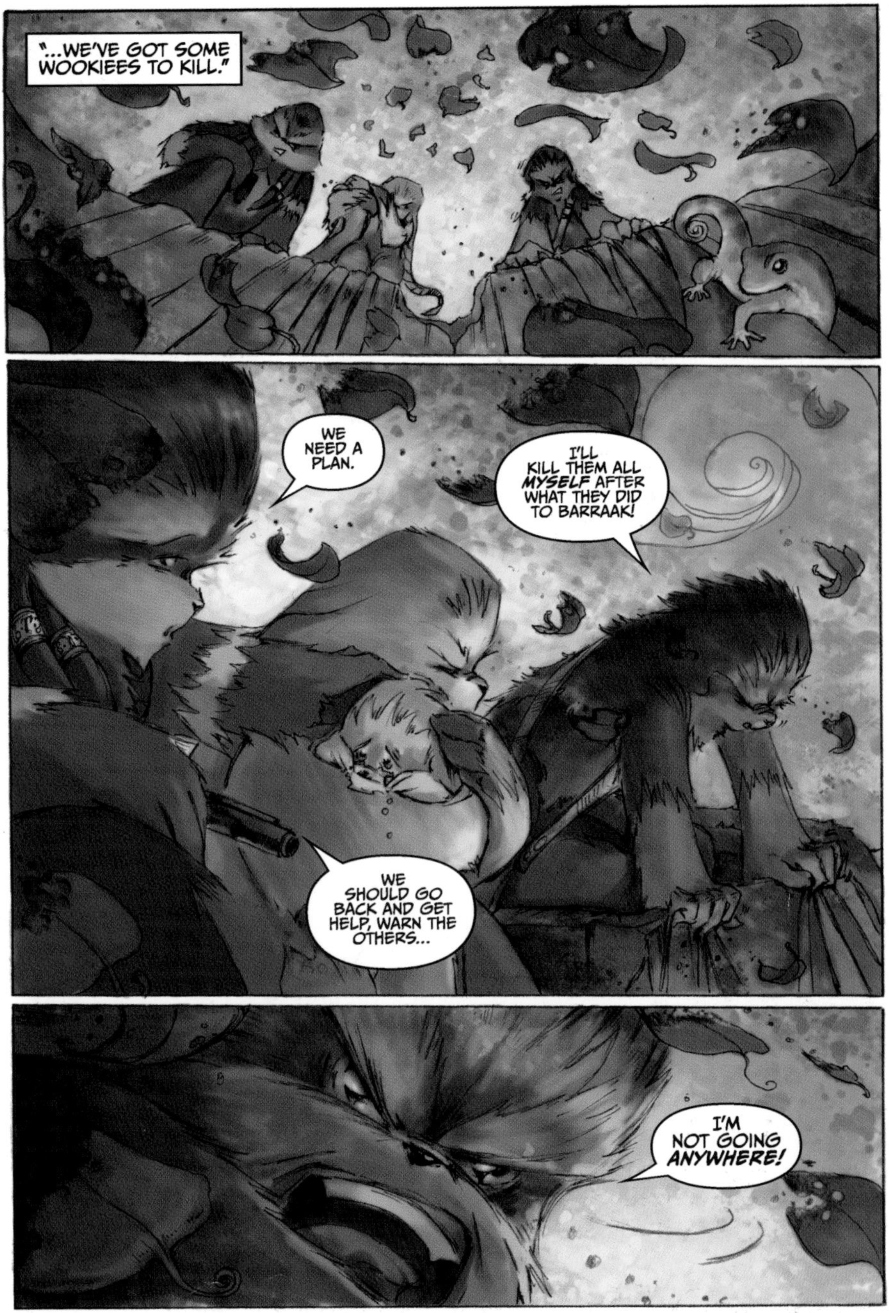
"...WE'VE GOT SOME WOOKIEES TO KILL."
WE NEED A PLAN.
I'LL KILL THEM ALL MYSELF AFTER WHAT THEY DID TO BARRAAK!
WE SHOULD GO BACK AND GET HELP, WARN THE OTHERS...
I'M NOT GOING ANYWHERE!

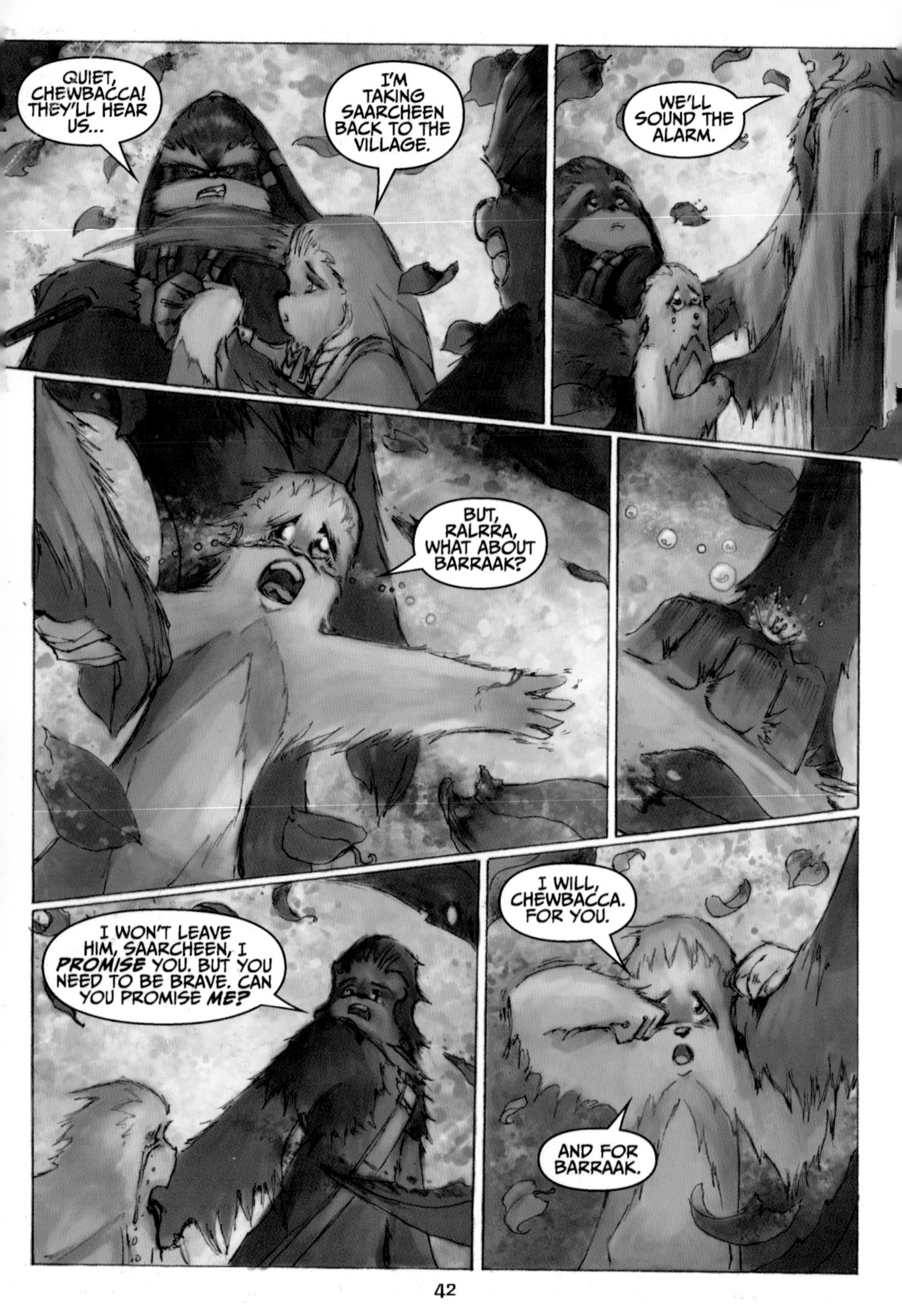
QUIET, CHEWBACCA! THEY'LL HEAR US...
I'M TAKING SAARCHEEN BACK TO THE VILLAGE.
WE'LL SOUND THE ALARM.
BUT, RALRRA, WHAT ABOUT BARRAAK?
I WON'T LEAVE HIM, SAARCHEEN, I ***PROMISE*** YOU. BUT YOU NEED TO BE BRAVE. CAN YOU PROMISE ***ME?***
I WILL, CHEWBACCA. FOR YOU.
AND FOR BARRAAK.

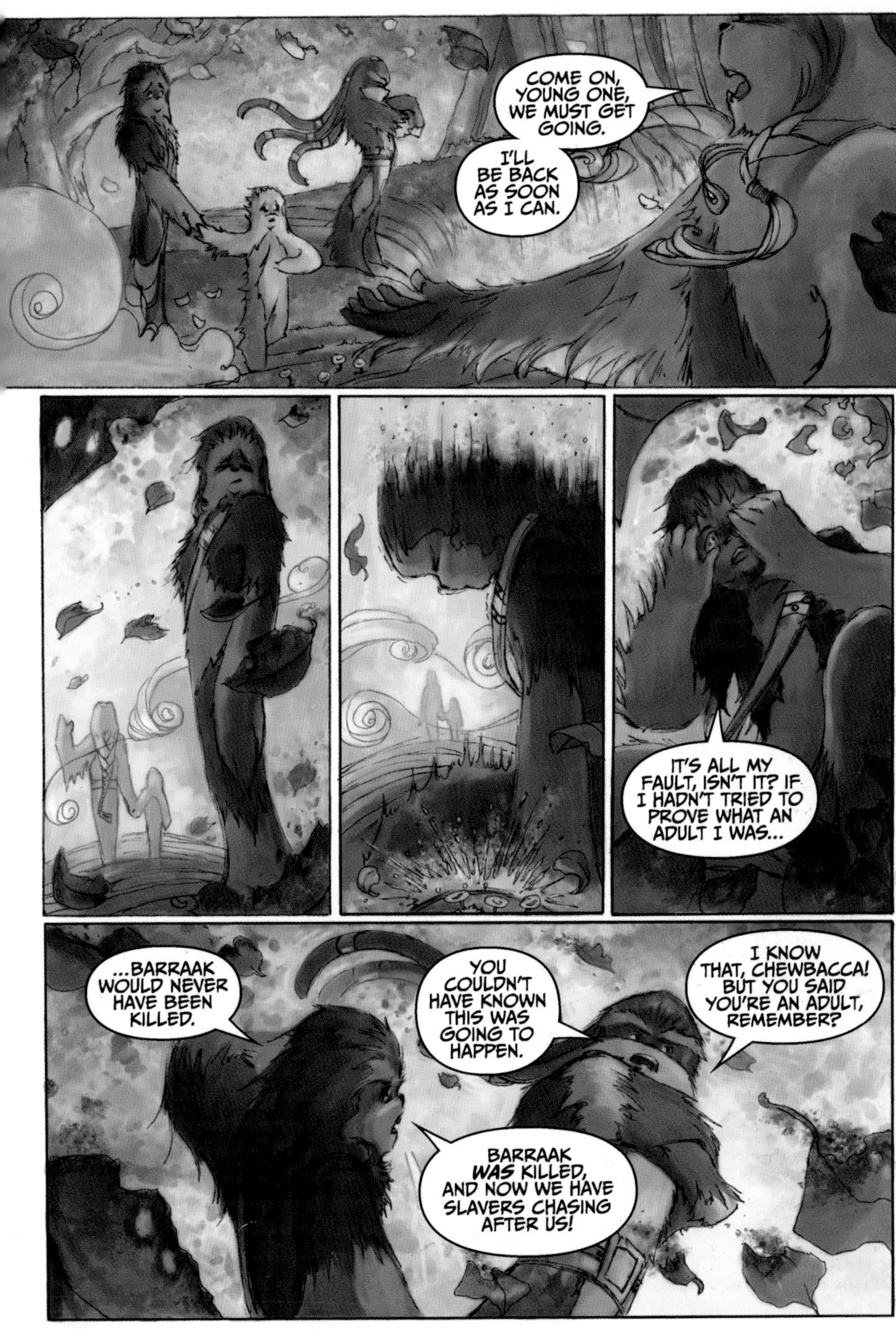
COME ON, YOUNG ONE, WE MUST GET GOING.
I'LL BE BACK AS SOON AS I CAN.
IT'S ALL MY FAULT, ISN'T IT? IF I HADN'T TRIED TO PROVE WHAT AN ADULT I WAS...
...BARRAAK WOULD NEVER HAVE BEEN KILLED.
YOU COULDN'T HAVE KNOWN THIS WAS GOING TO HAPPEN.
I KNOW THAT, CHEWBACCA! BUT YOU SAID YOU'RE AN ADULT, REMEMBER?
BARRAAK *WAS* KILLED, AND NOW WE HAVE SLAVERS CHASING AFTER US!

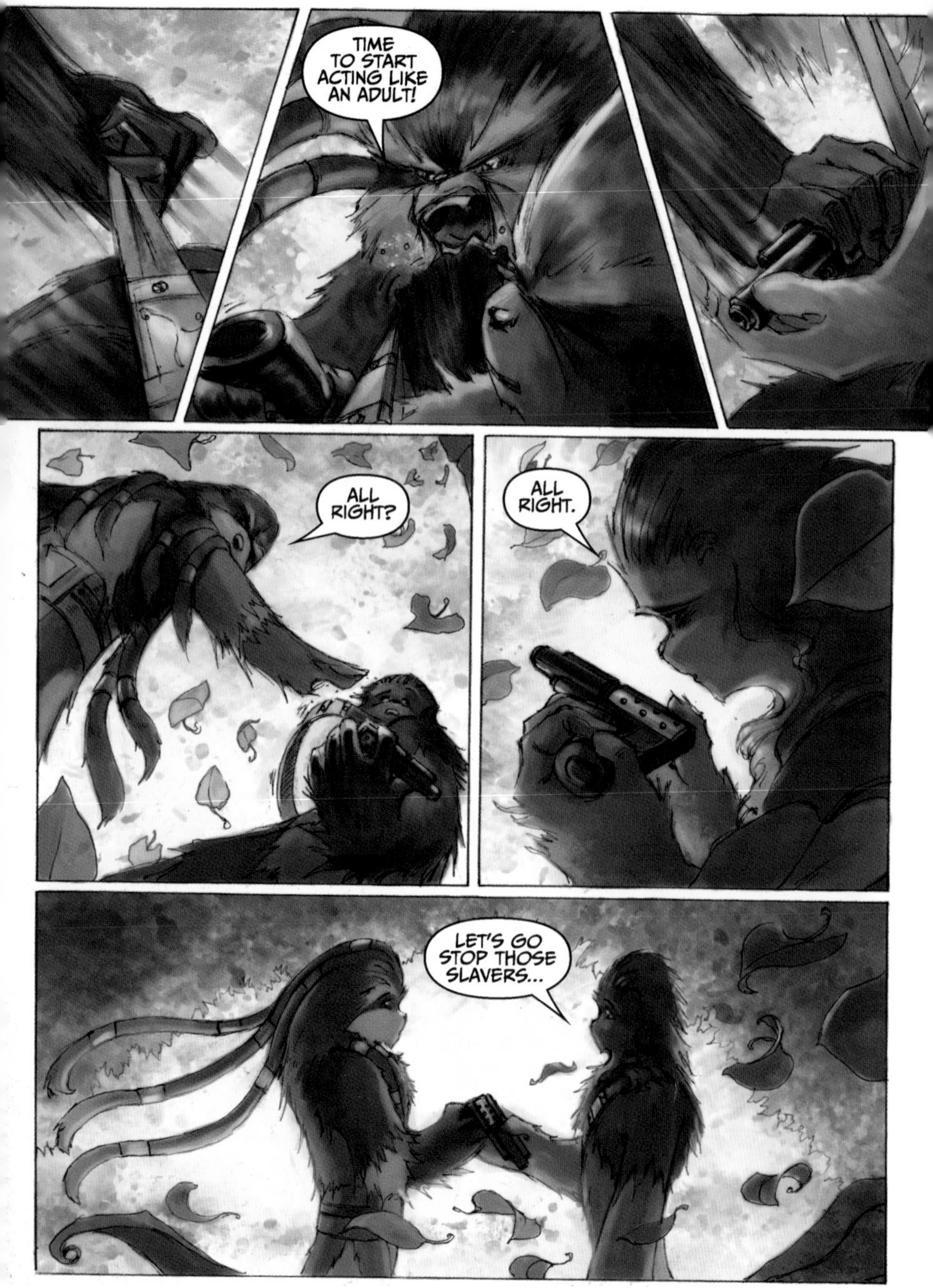
TIME TO START ACTING LIKE AN ADULT!
ALL RIGHT?
ALL RIGHT.
LET'S GO STOP THOSE SLAVERS...

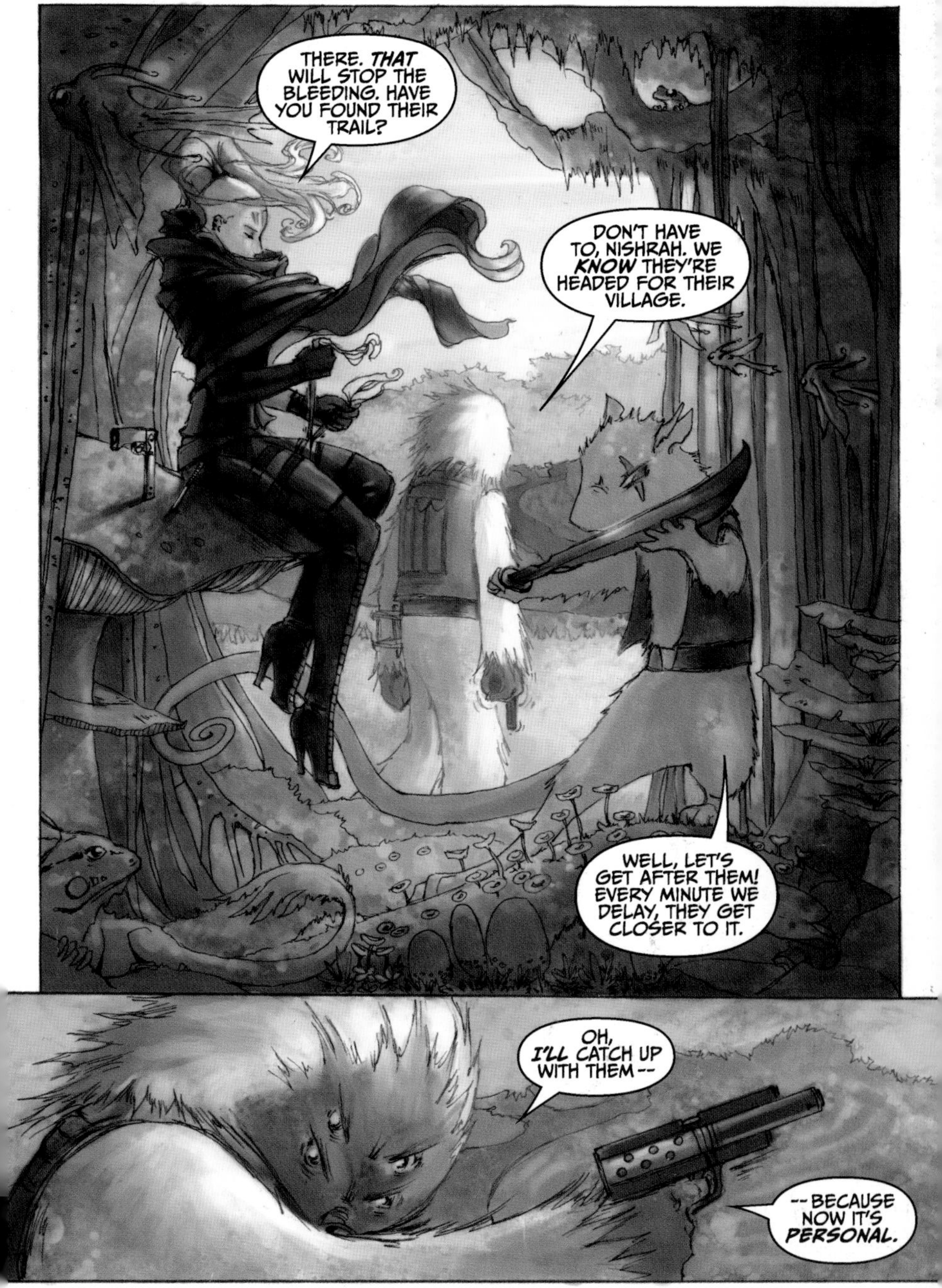
THERE. THAT WILL STOP THE BLEEDING. HAVE YOU FOUND THEIR TRAIL?
DON'T HAVE TO, NISHRAH. WE KNOW THEY'RE HEADED FOR THEIR VILLAGE.
WELL, LET'S GET AFTER THEM! EVERY MINUTE WE DELAY, THEY GET CLOSER TO IT.
OH, I'LL CATCH UP WITH THEM --
-- BECAUSE NOW IT'S PERSONAL.

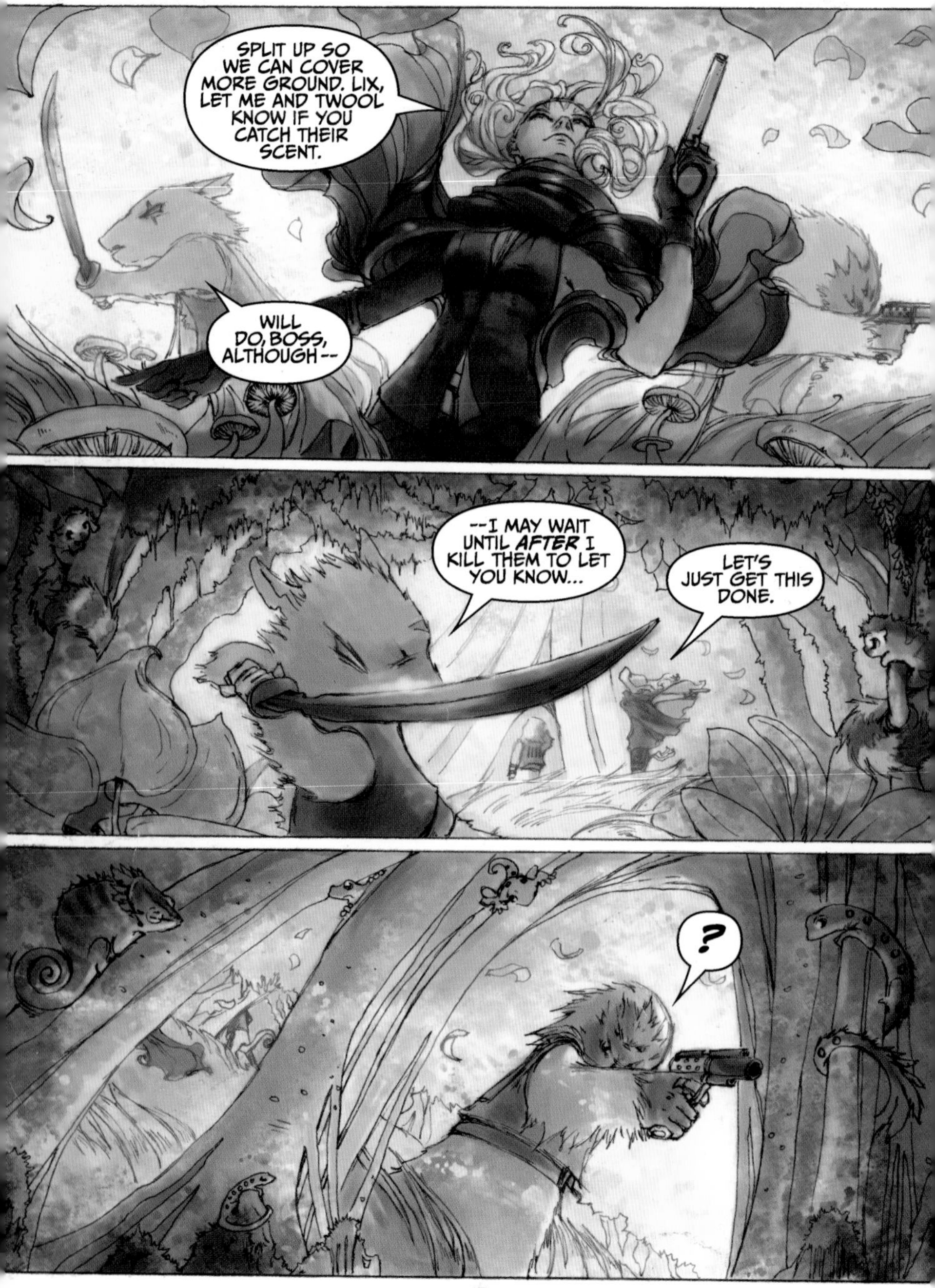
SPLIT UP SO WE CAN COVER MORE GROUND. LIX, LET ME AND TWOOL KNOW IF YOU CATCH THEIR SCENT.
WILL DO, BOSS, ALTHOUGH--
--I MAY WAIT UNTIL *AFTER* I KILL THEM TO LET YOU KNOW...
LET'S JUST GET THIS DONE.
?

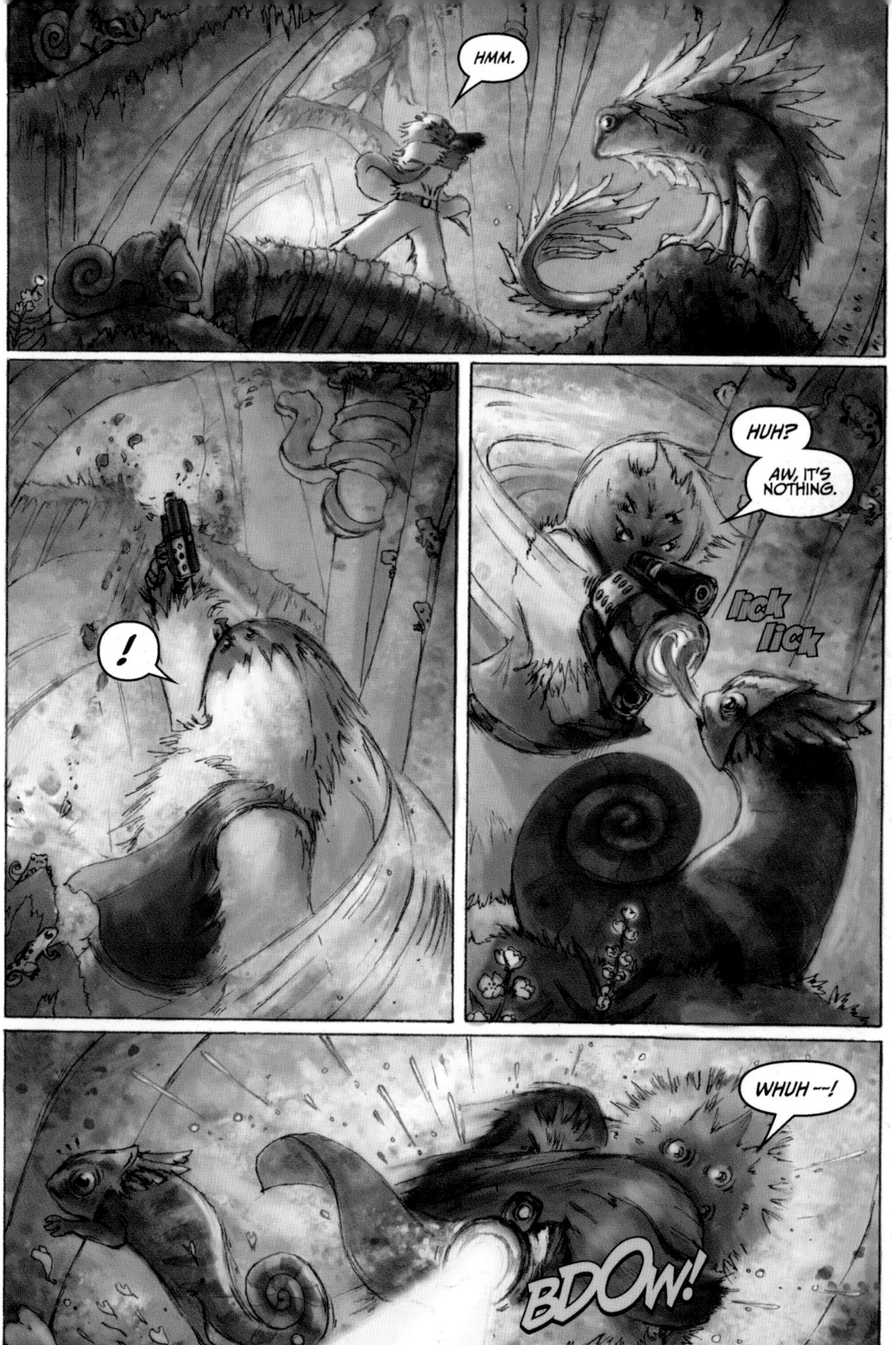

HMM.
!
HUH?
AW, IT'S NOTHING.
lick lick
WHUH --!
BDOW!

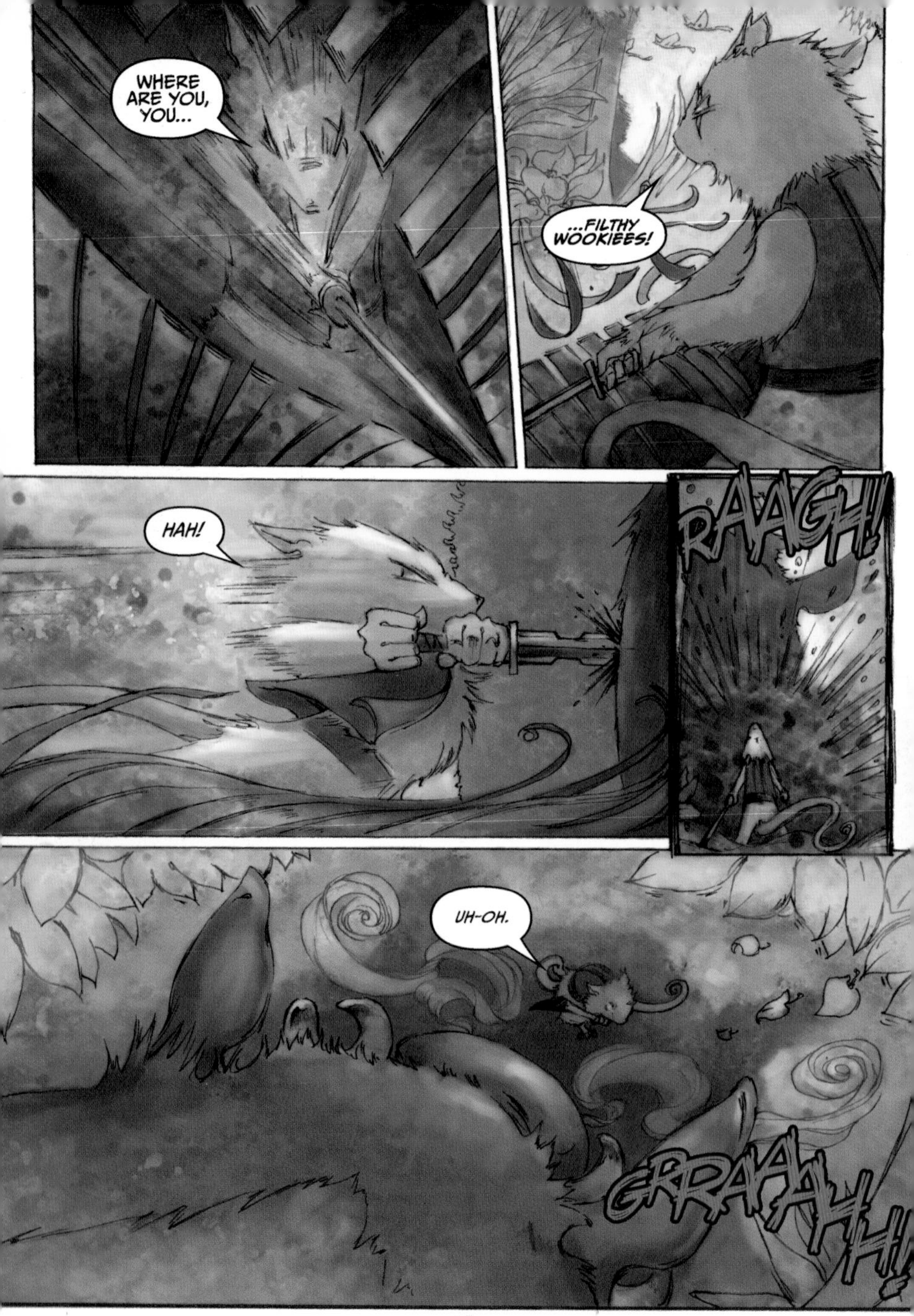
WHERE ARE YOU, YOU...
...FILTHY WOOKIEES!
HAH!
RAAGH!!
UH-OH.
GRRAAAHH!

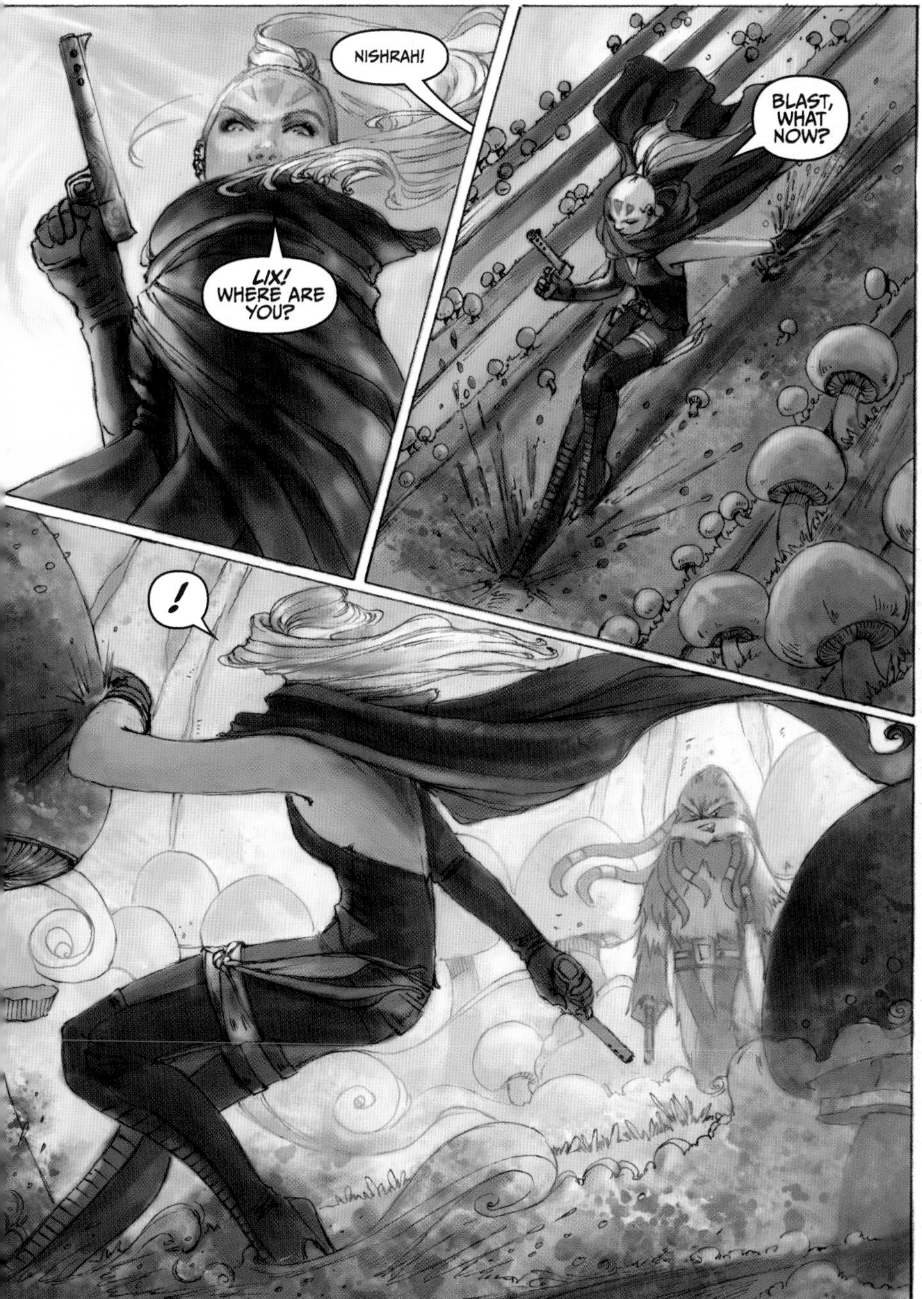
NISHRAH!
LIX! WHERE ARE YOU?
BLAST, WHAT NOW?
!

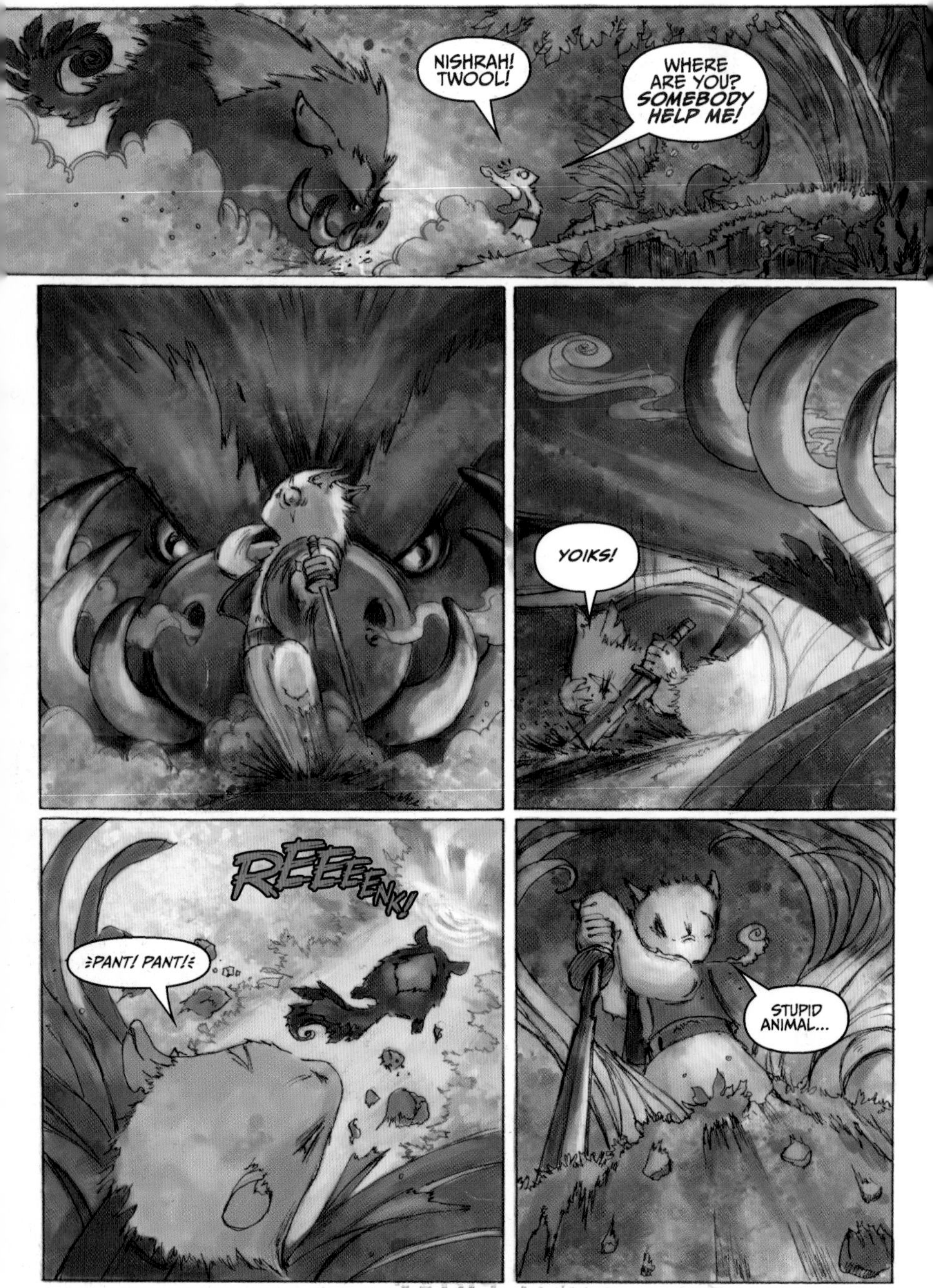
NISHRAH! TWOOL!
WHERE ARE YOU? SOMEBODY HELP ME!
YOIKS!
REEEEENK!
PANT! PANT!
STUPID ANIMAL...

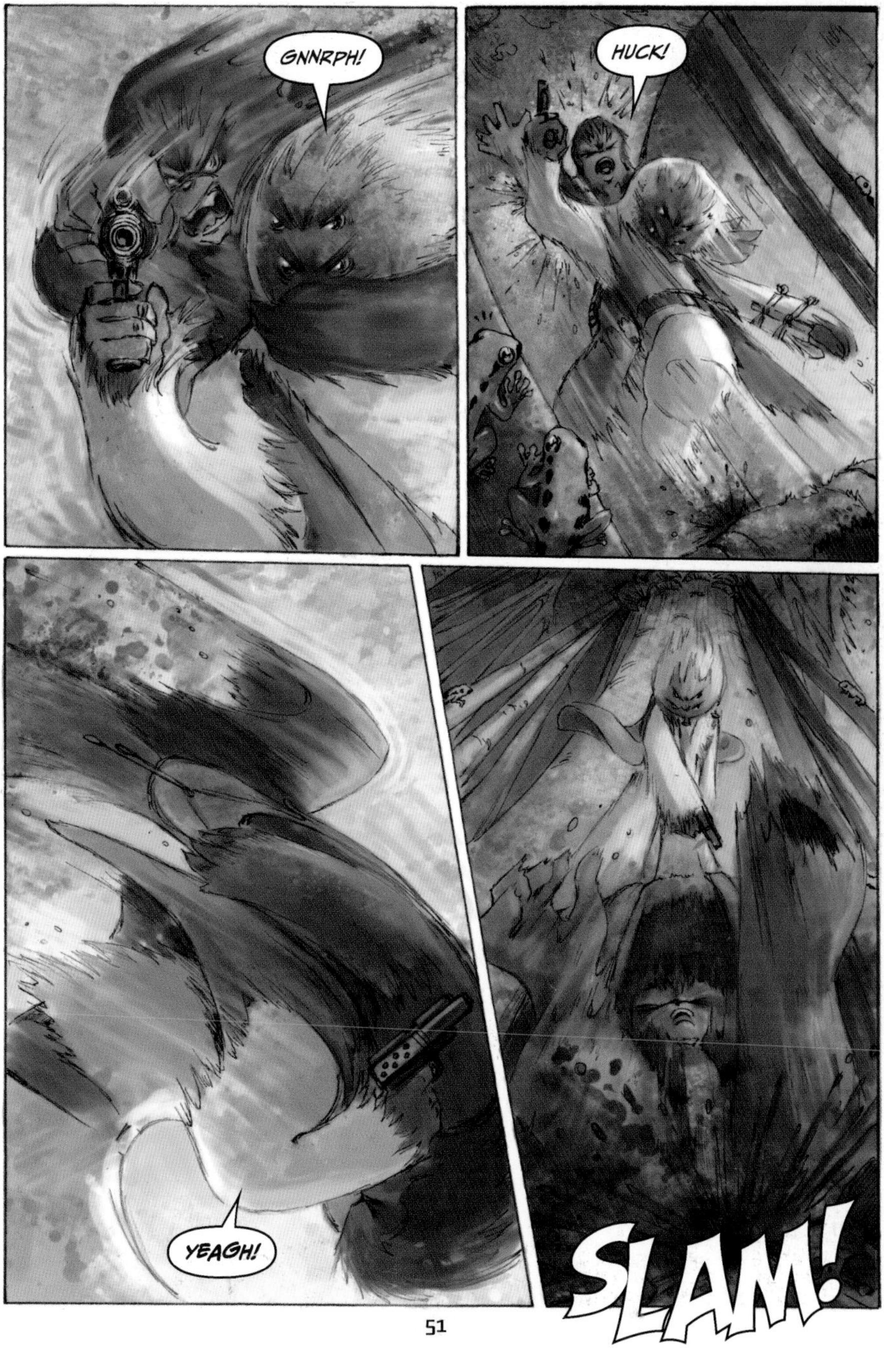
GNNRPH!
HUCK!
YEAGH!
SLAM!

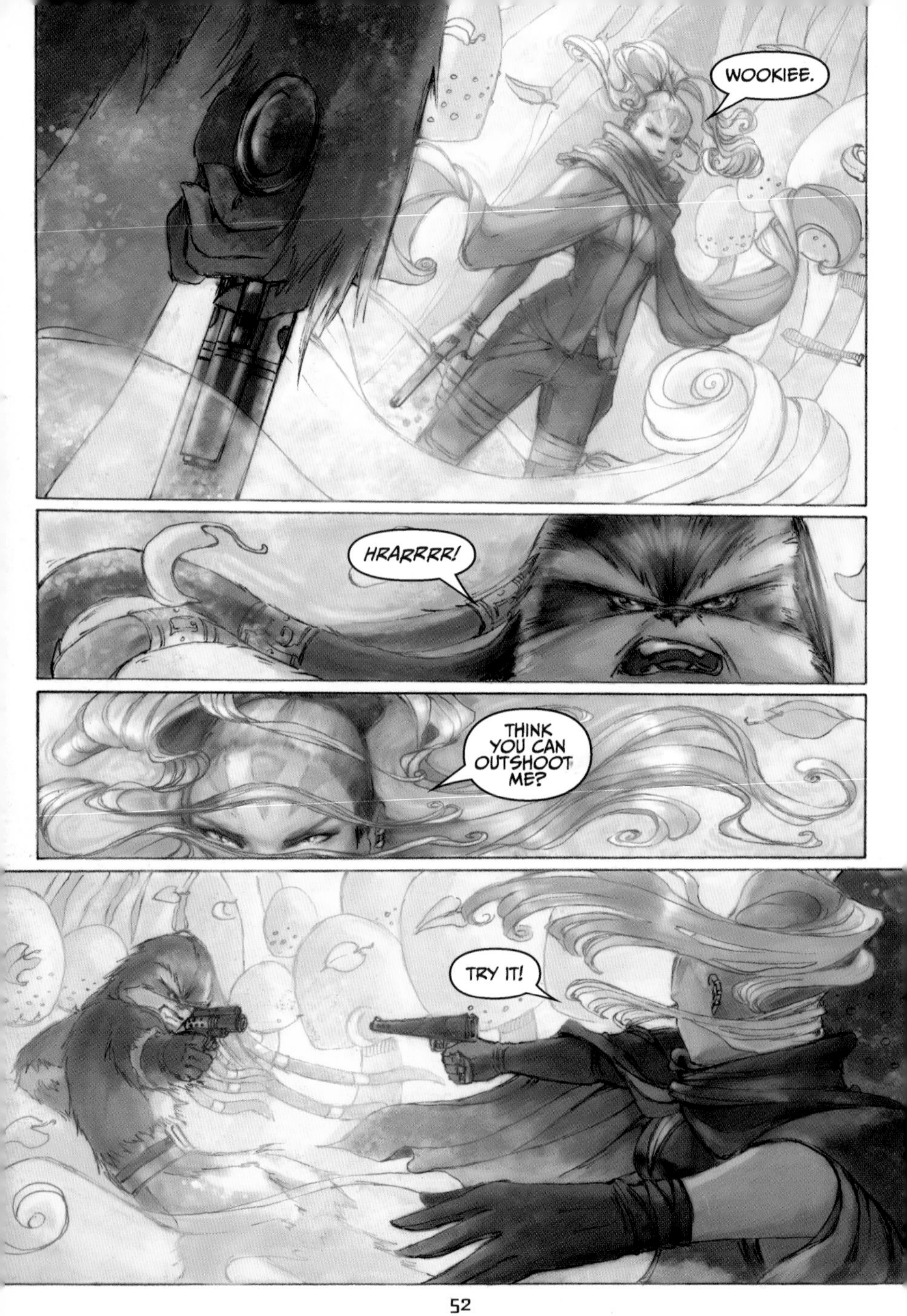
WOOKIEE.
HRARRRR!
THINK YOU CAN OUTSHOOT ME?
TRY IT!

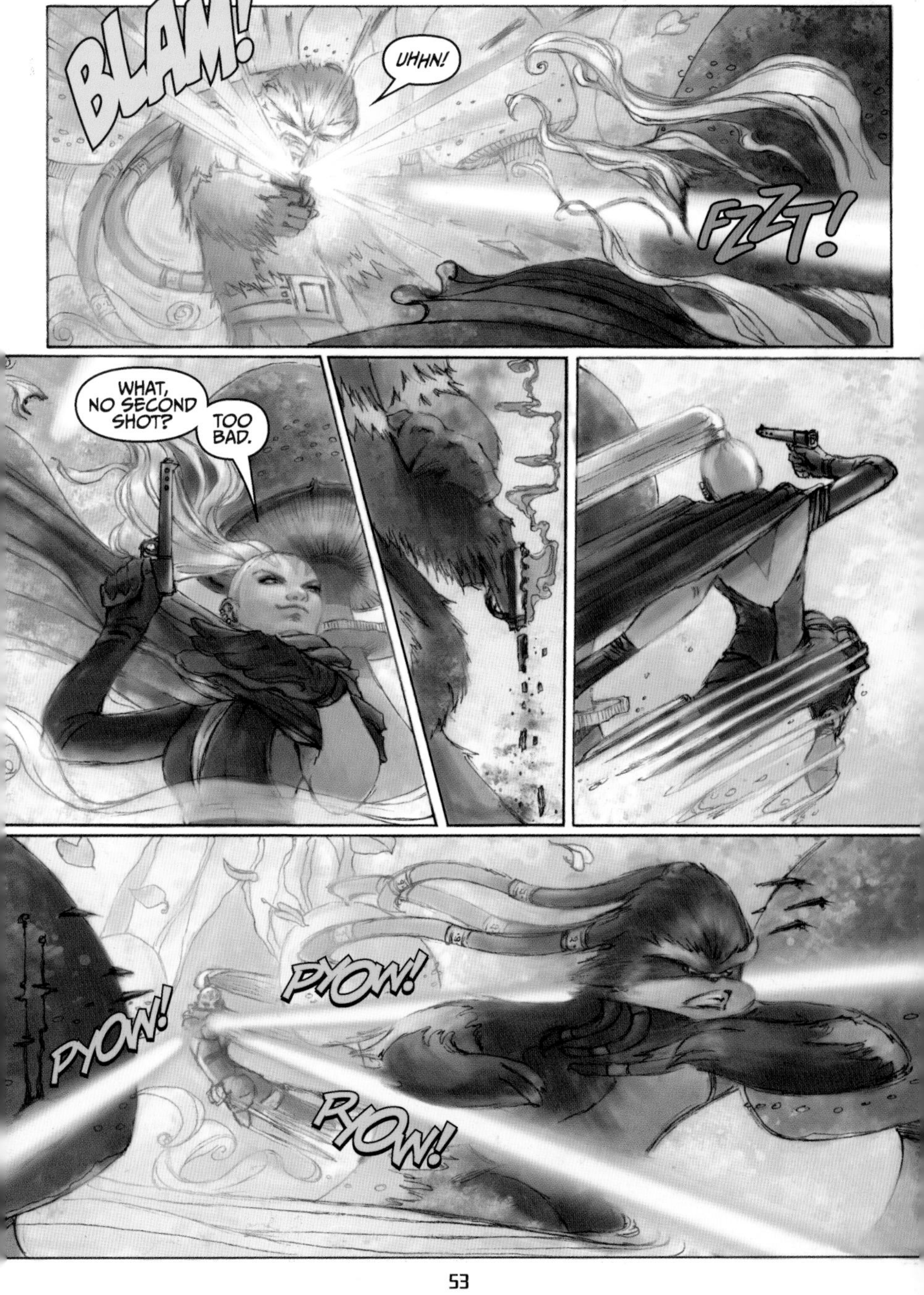
BLAM!
UHHN!
FZZT!
WHAT, NO SECOND SHOT?
TOO BAD.
PYOW!
PYOW!
PYOW!

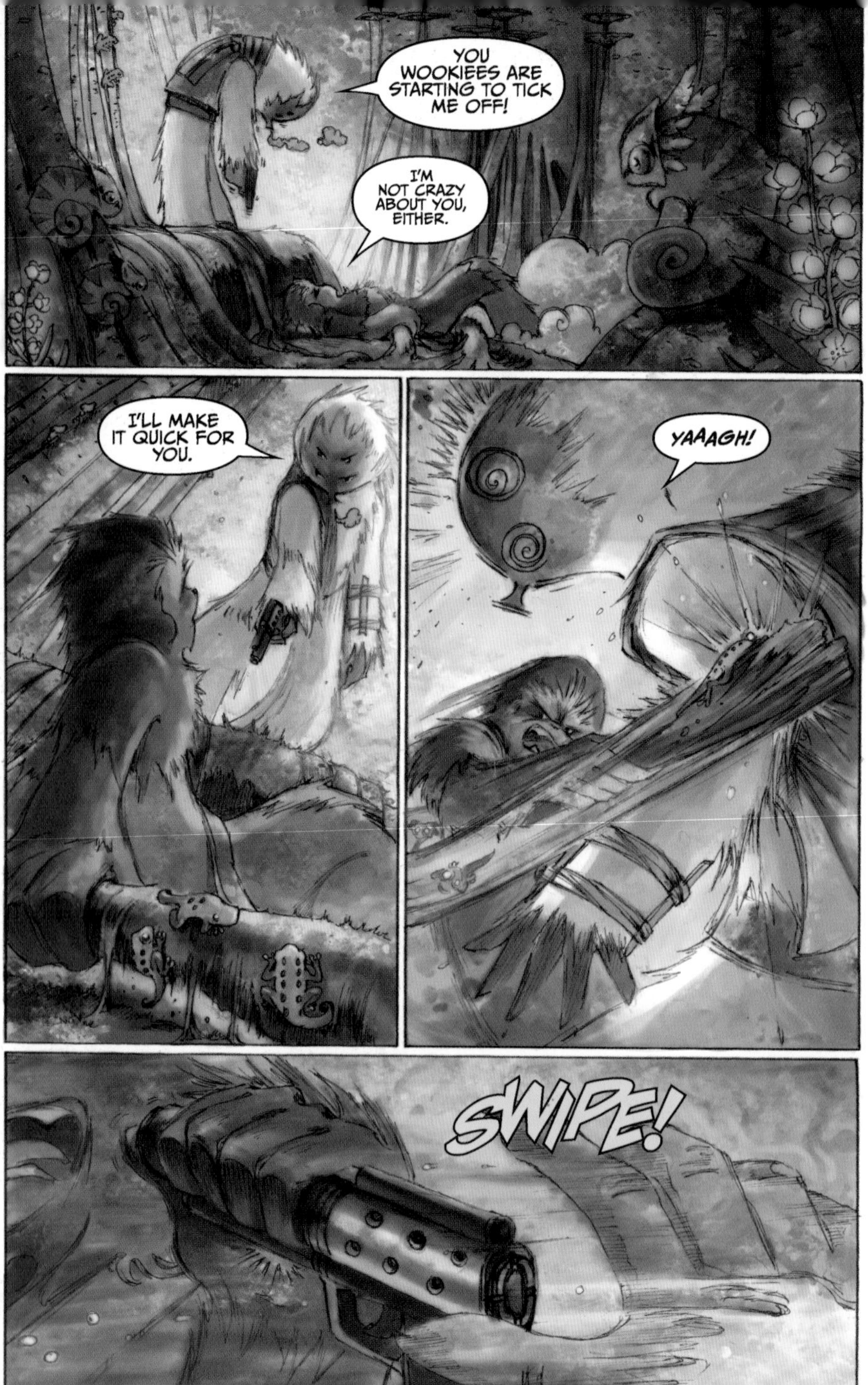
YOU WOOKIEES ARE STARTING TO TICK ME OFF!
I'M NOT CRAZY ABOUT YOU, EITHER.
I'LL MAKE IT QUICK FOR YOU.
YAAAGH!
SWIPE!

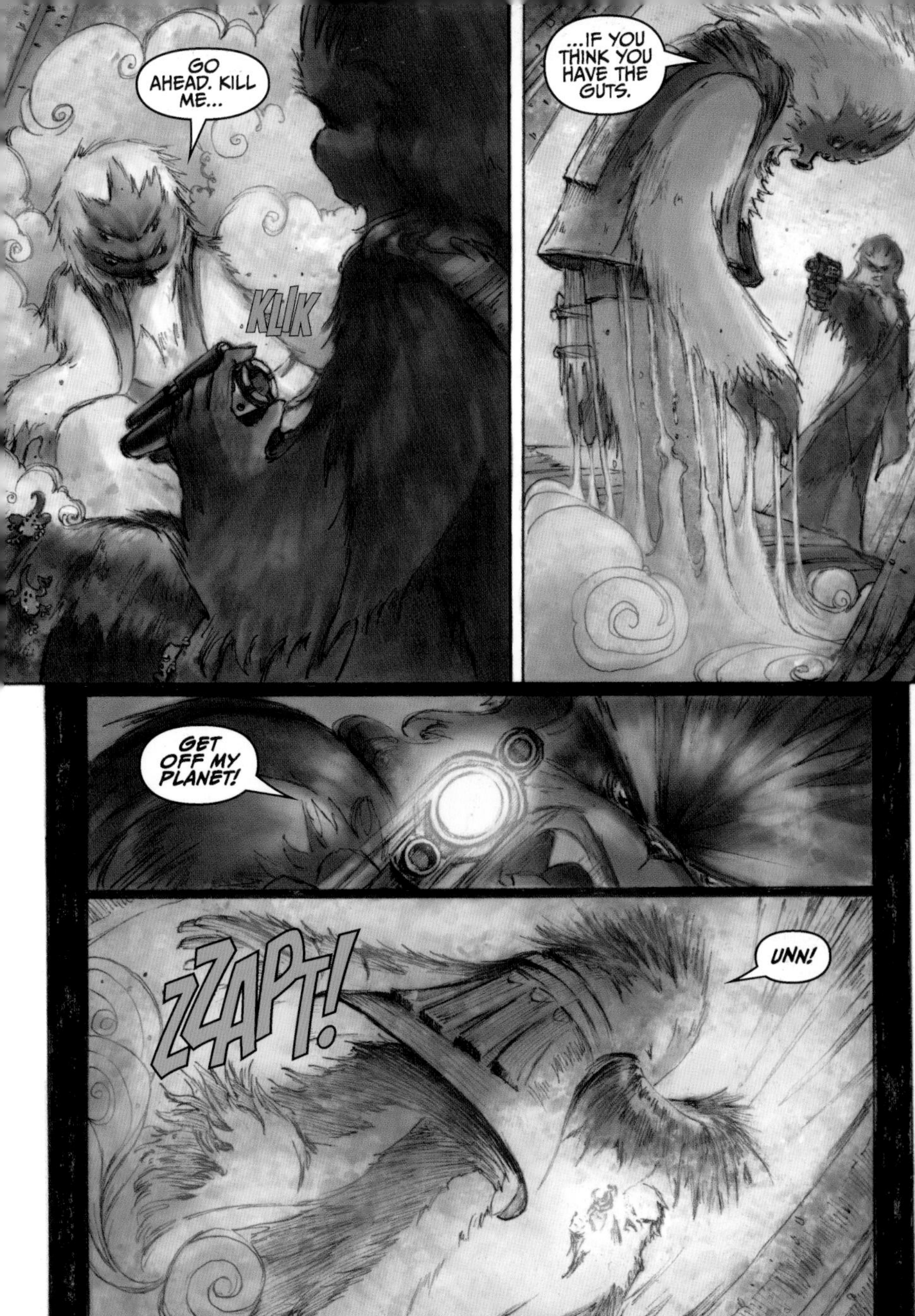
GO AHEAD. KILL ME...
KLIK
...IF YOU THINK YOU HAVE THE GUTS.
GET OFF MY PLANET!
ZZAPT!
UNN!

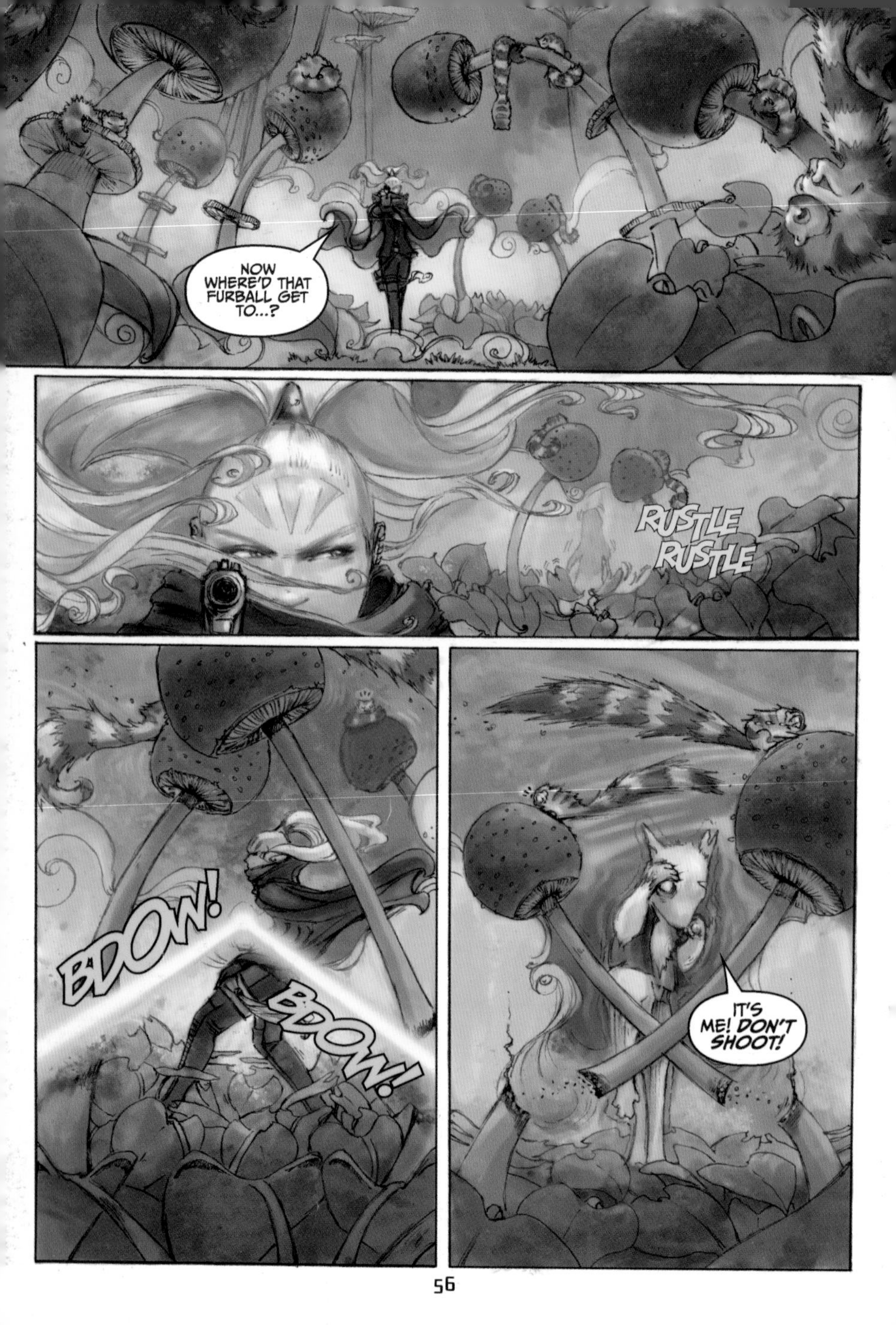
NOW WHERE'D THAT FURBALL GET TO...?
RUSTLE RUSTLE
BDOW!
BDOW!
IT'S ME! DON'T SHOOT!

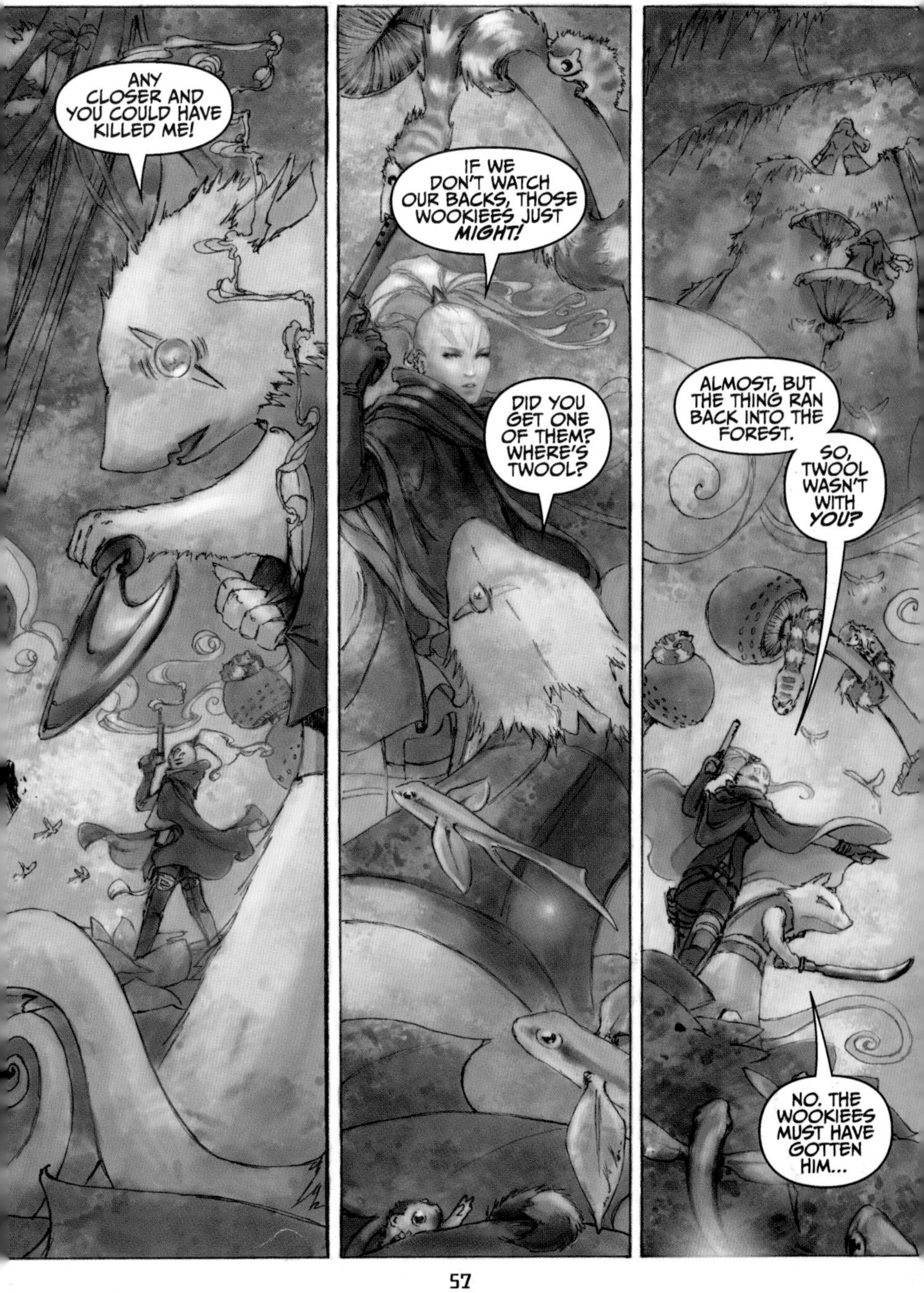
ANY CLOSER AND YOU COULD HAVE KILLED ME!
IF WE DON'T WATCH OUR BACKS, THOSE WOOKIEES JUST *MIGHT!*
DID YOU GET ONE OF THEM? WHERE'S TWOOL?
ALMOST, BUT THE THING RAN BACK INTO THE FOREST.
SO, TWOOL WASN'T WITH *YOU?*
NO. THE WOOKIEES MUST HAVE GOTTEN HIM...

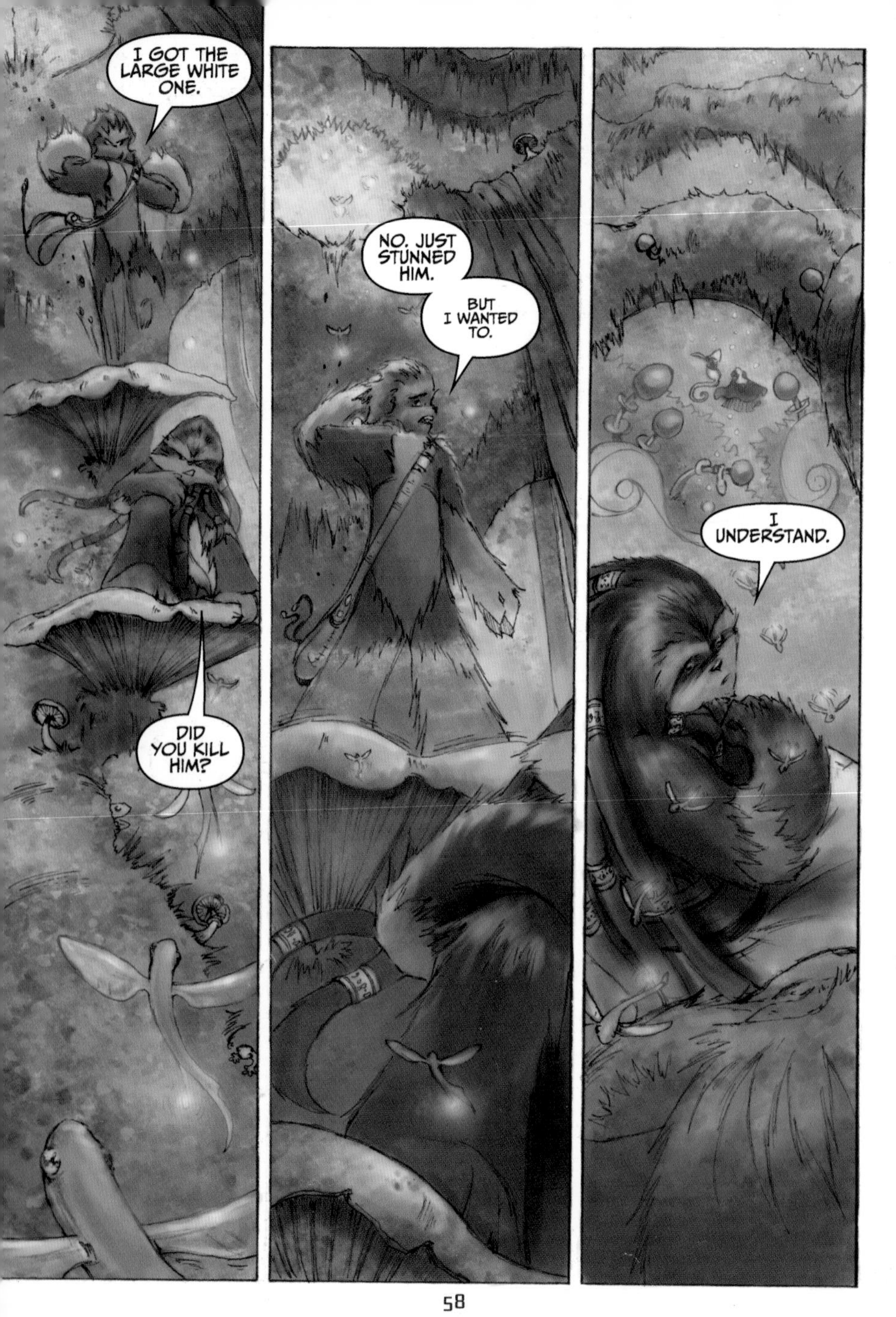
I GOT THE LARGE WHITE ONE.
DID YOU KILL HIM?
NO. JUST STUNNED HIM.
BUT I WANTED TO.
I UNDERSTAND.

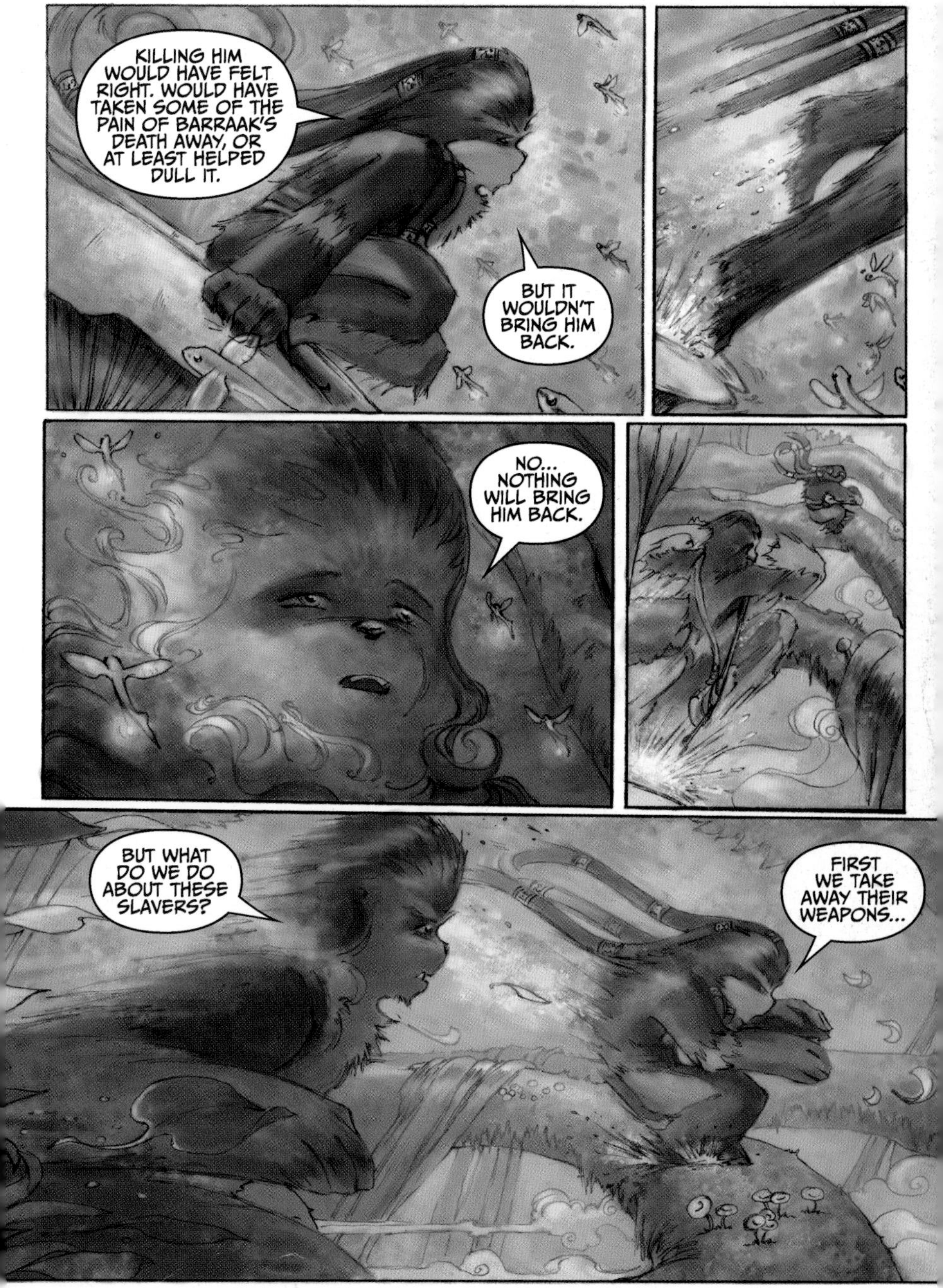
KILLING HIM WOULD HAVE FELT RIGHT. WOULD HAVE TAKEN SOME OF THE PAIN OF BARRAAK'S DEATH AWAY, OR AT LEAST HELPED DULL IT.
BUT IT WOULDN'T BRING HIM BACK.
NO... NOTHING WILL BRING HIM BACK.
BUT WHAT DO WE DO ABOUT THESE SLAVERS?
FIRST WE TAKE AWAY THEIR WEAPONS...

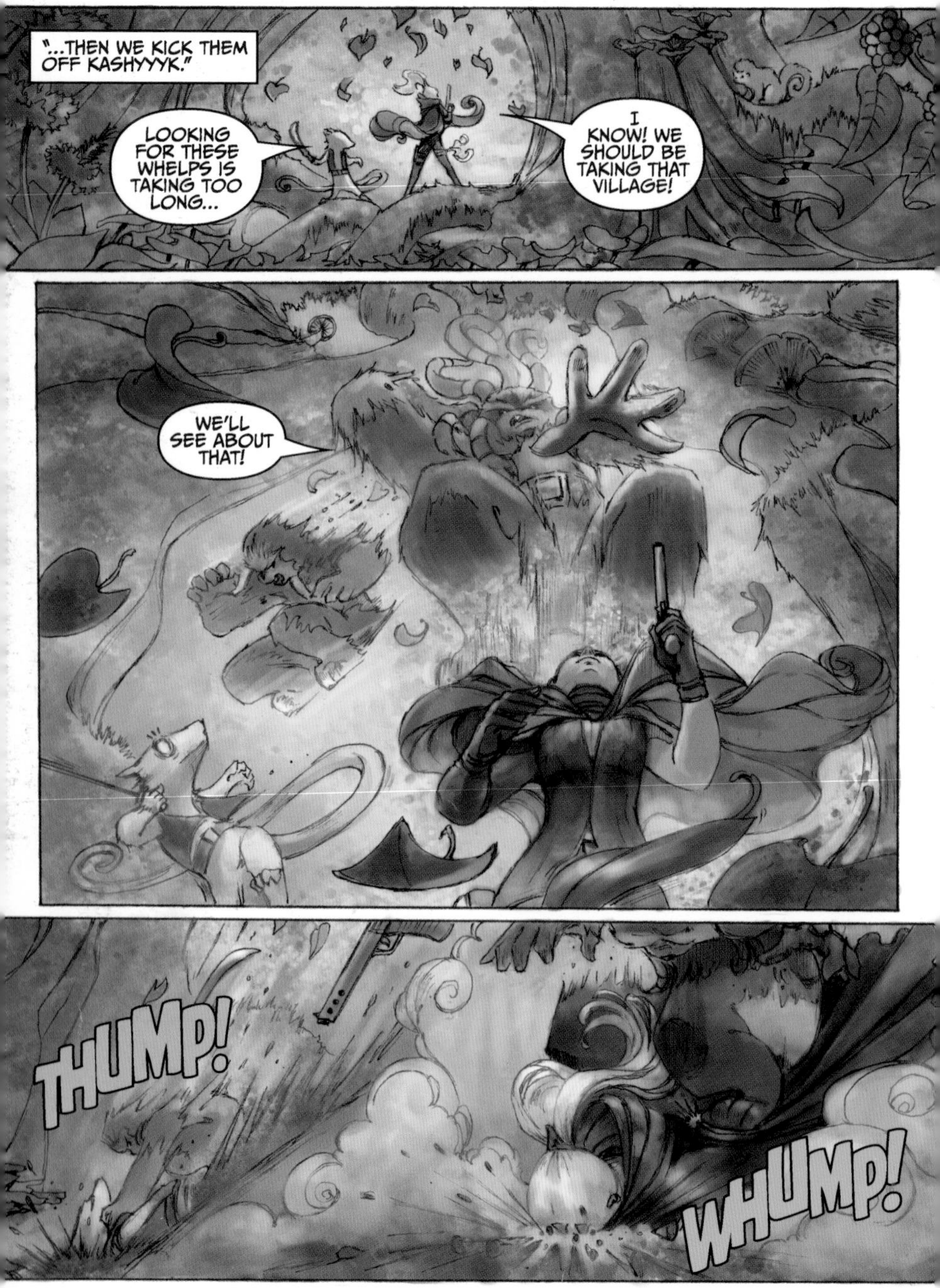
"...THEN WE KICK THEM OFF KASHYYYK."
LOOKING FOR THESE WHELPS IS TAKING TOO LONG...
I KNOW! WE SHOULD BE TAKING THAT VILLAGE!
WE'LL SEE ABOUT THAT!
THUMP!
WHUMP!

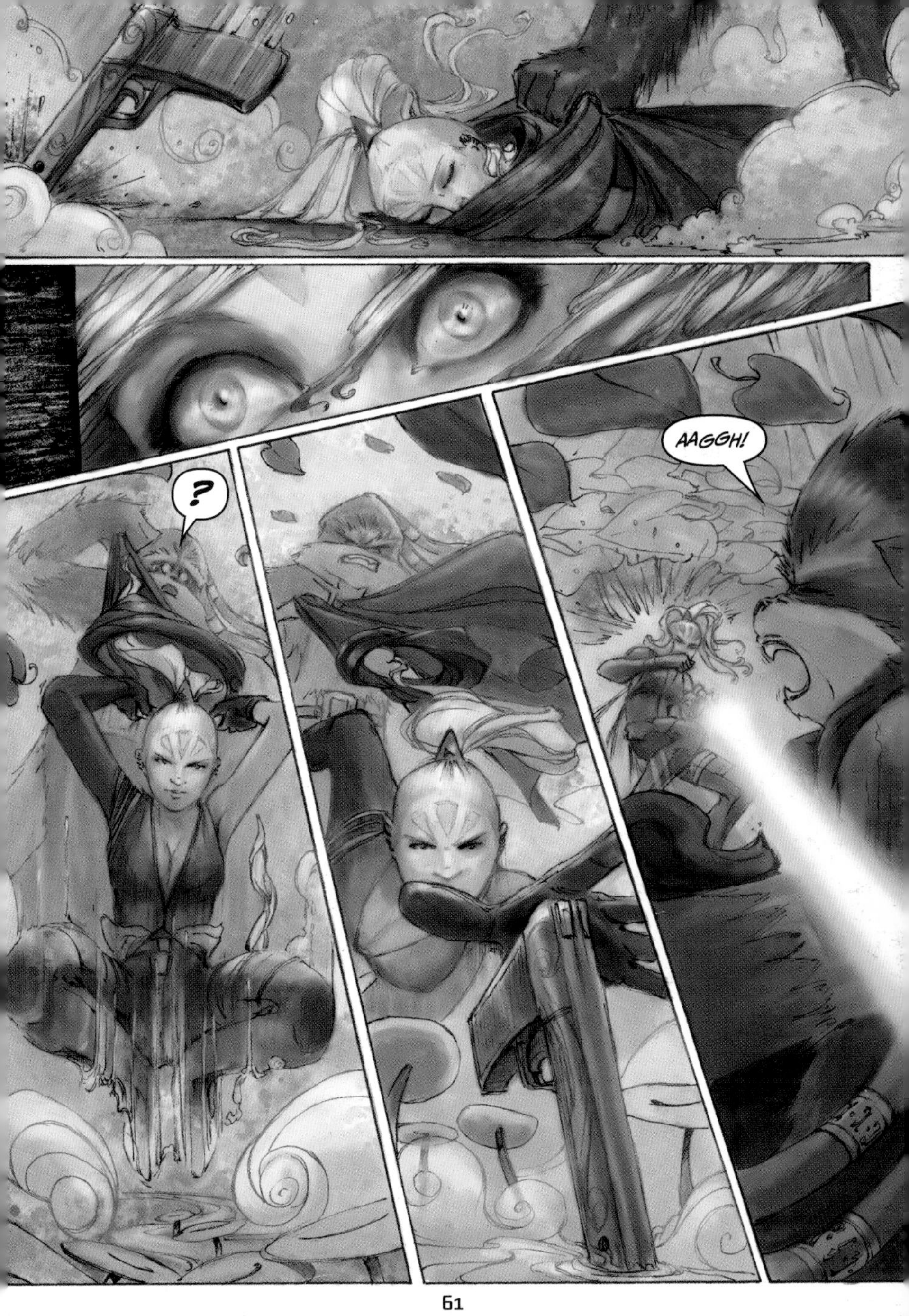
?
AAGGH!

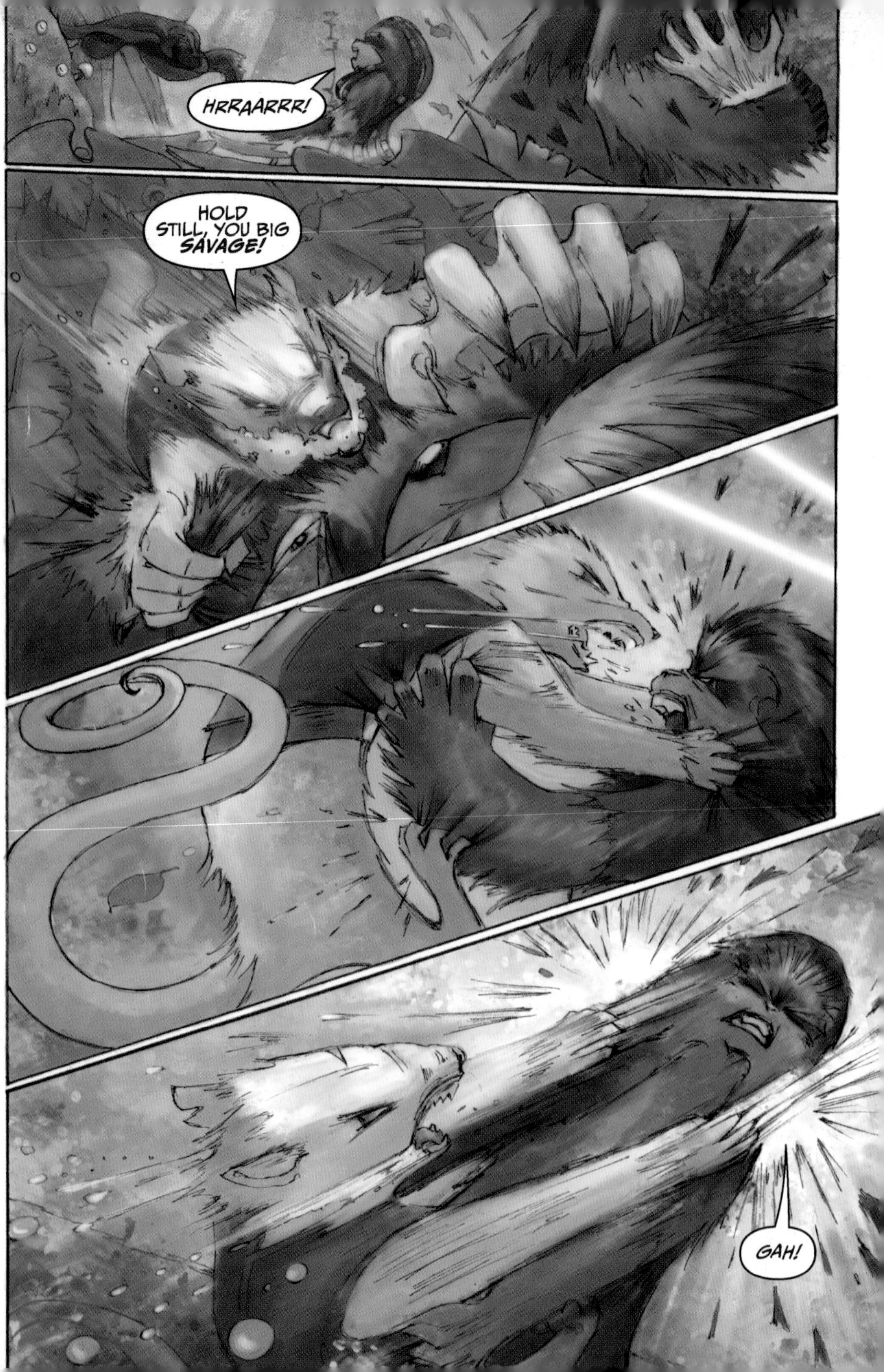
HRRAARRR!
HOLD STILL, YOU BIG SAVAGE!
GAH!

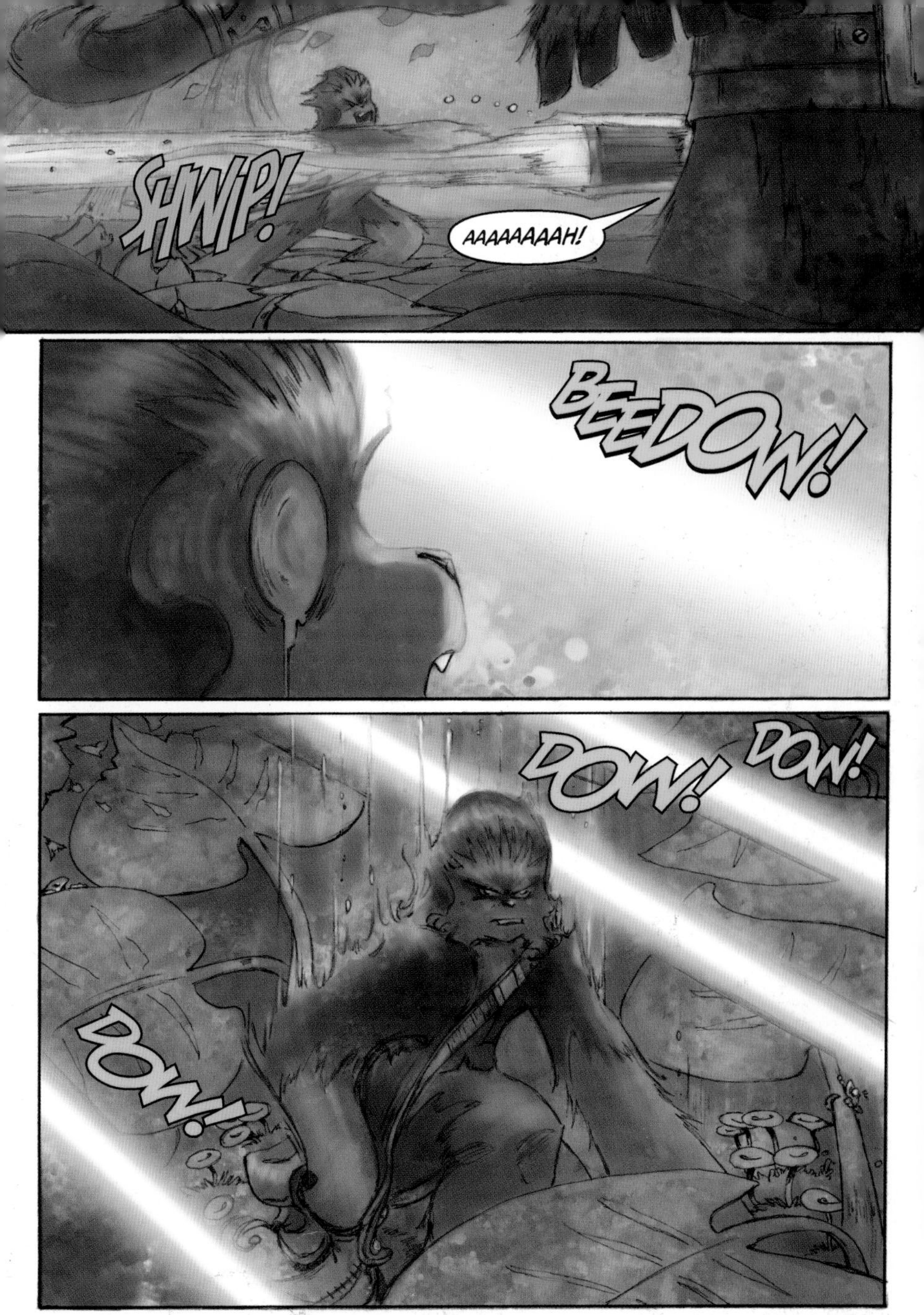
SHWIP!
AAAAAAAAH!
BEEDOW!
DOW!
DOW!
DOW!

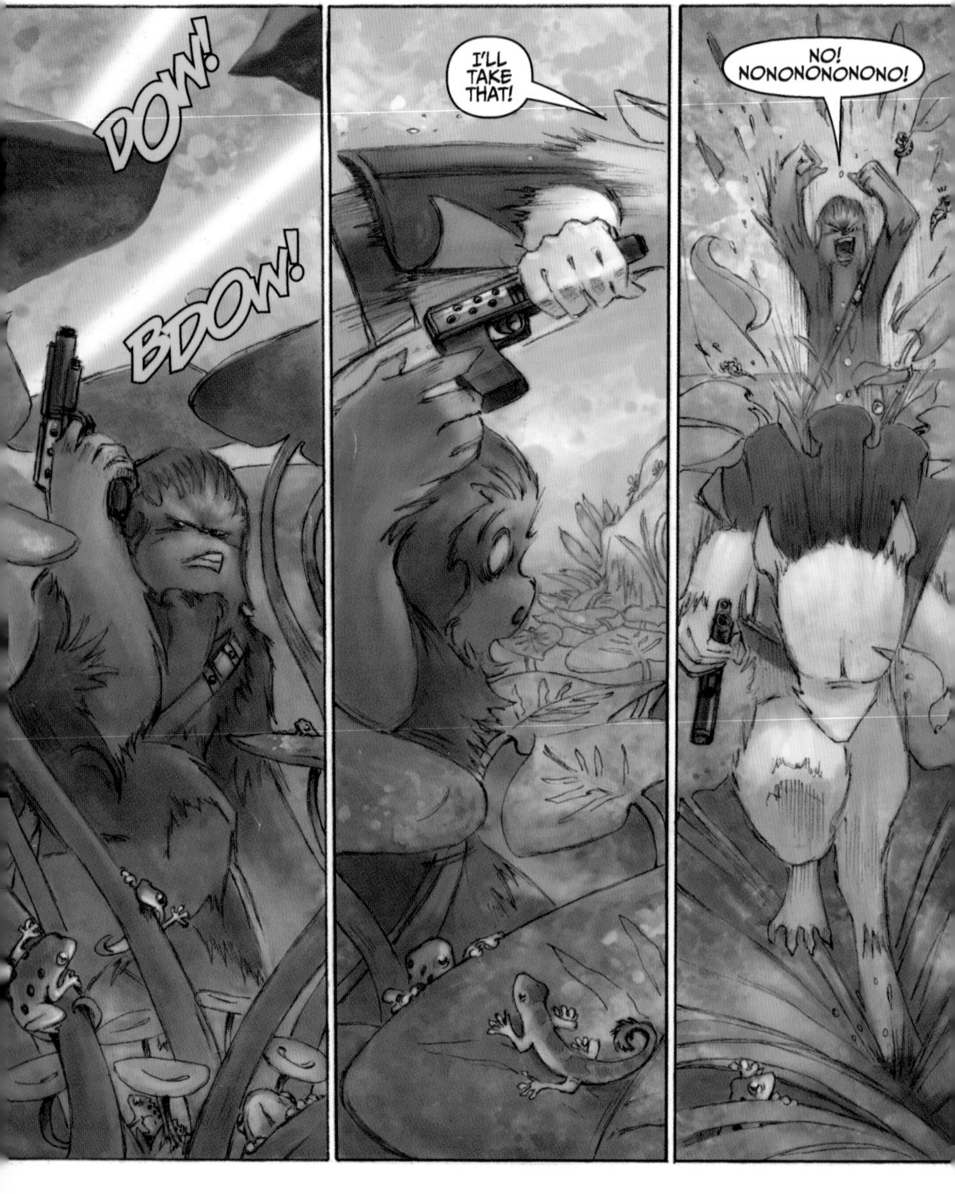
DOW!
BDOW!
I'LL TAKE THAT!
NO! NONONONONONO!

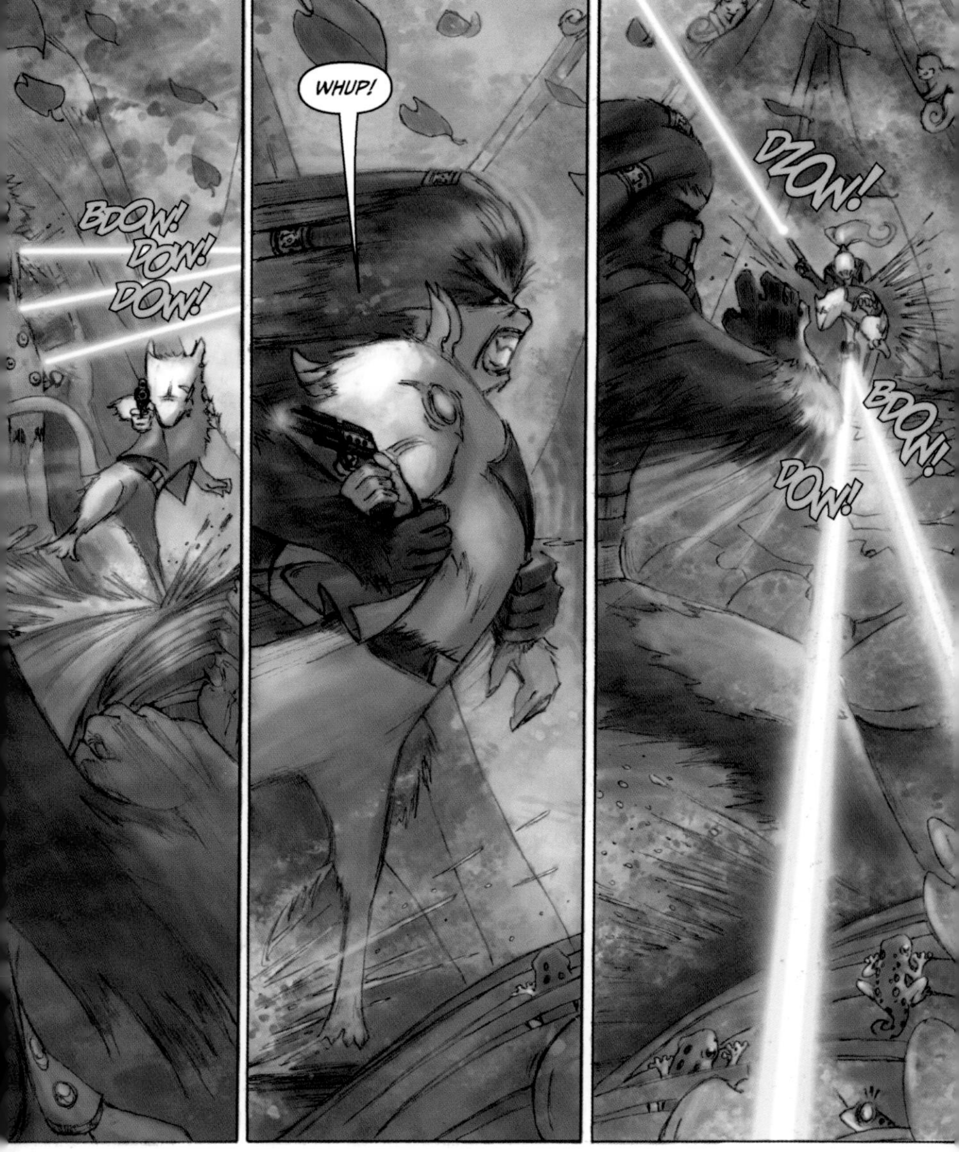
BDOW! DOW! DOW!
WHUP!
DZOW!
BDOW! DOW!

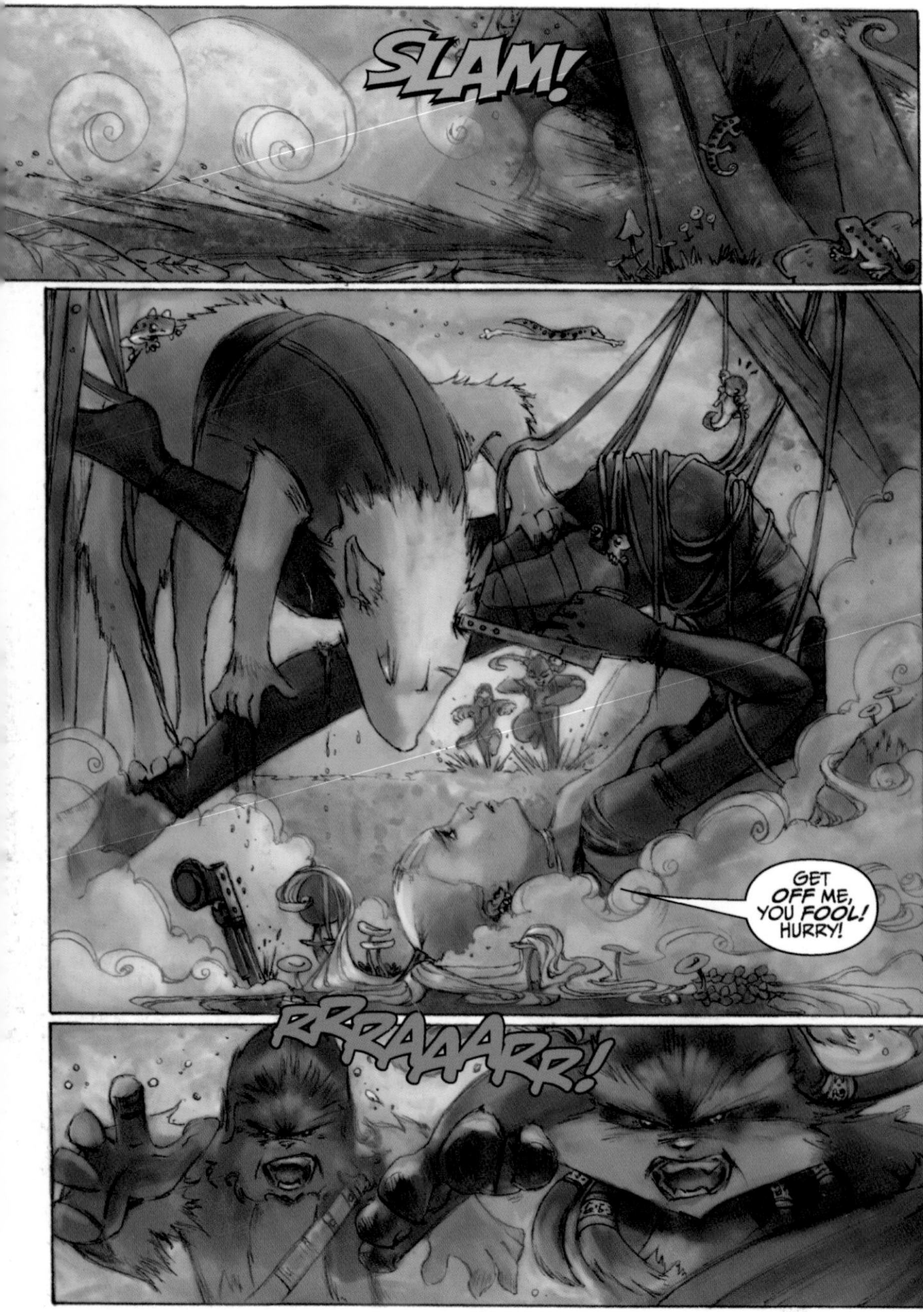
SLAM!
GET OFF ME, YOU FOOL! HURRY!
RRRAAAARR!

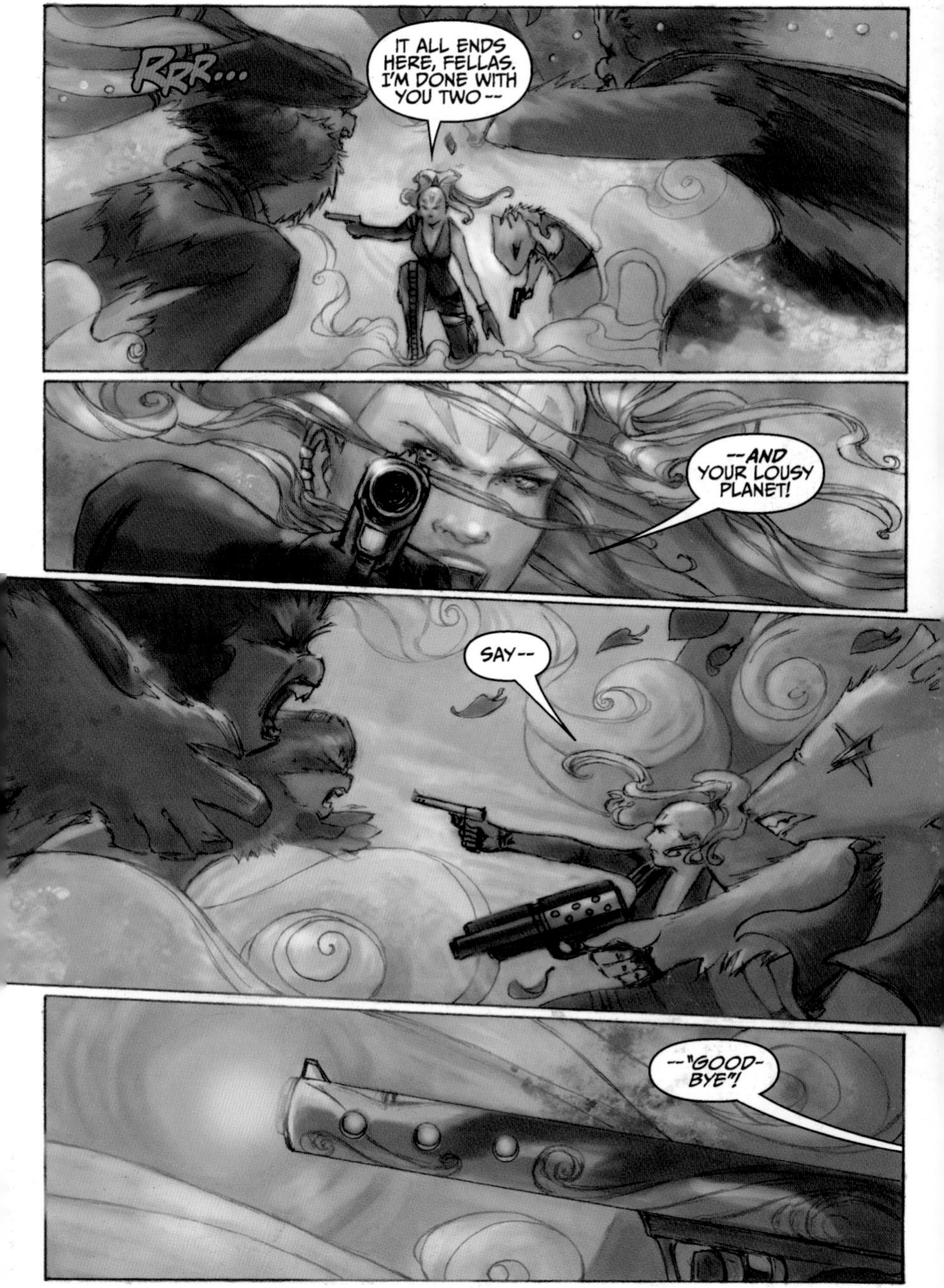
RRR...
IT ALL ENDS HERE, FELLAS. I'M DONE WITH YOU TWO--
--AND YOUR LOUSY PLANET!
SAY--
--"GOOD-BYE"!

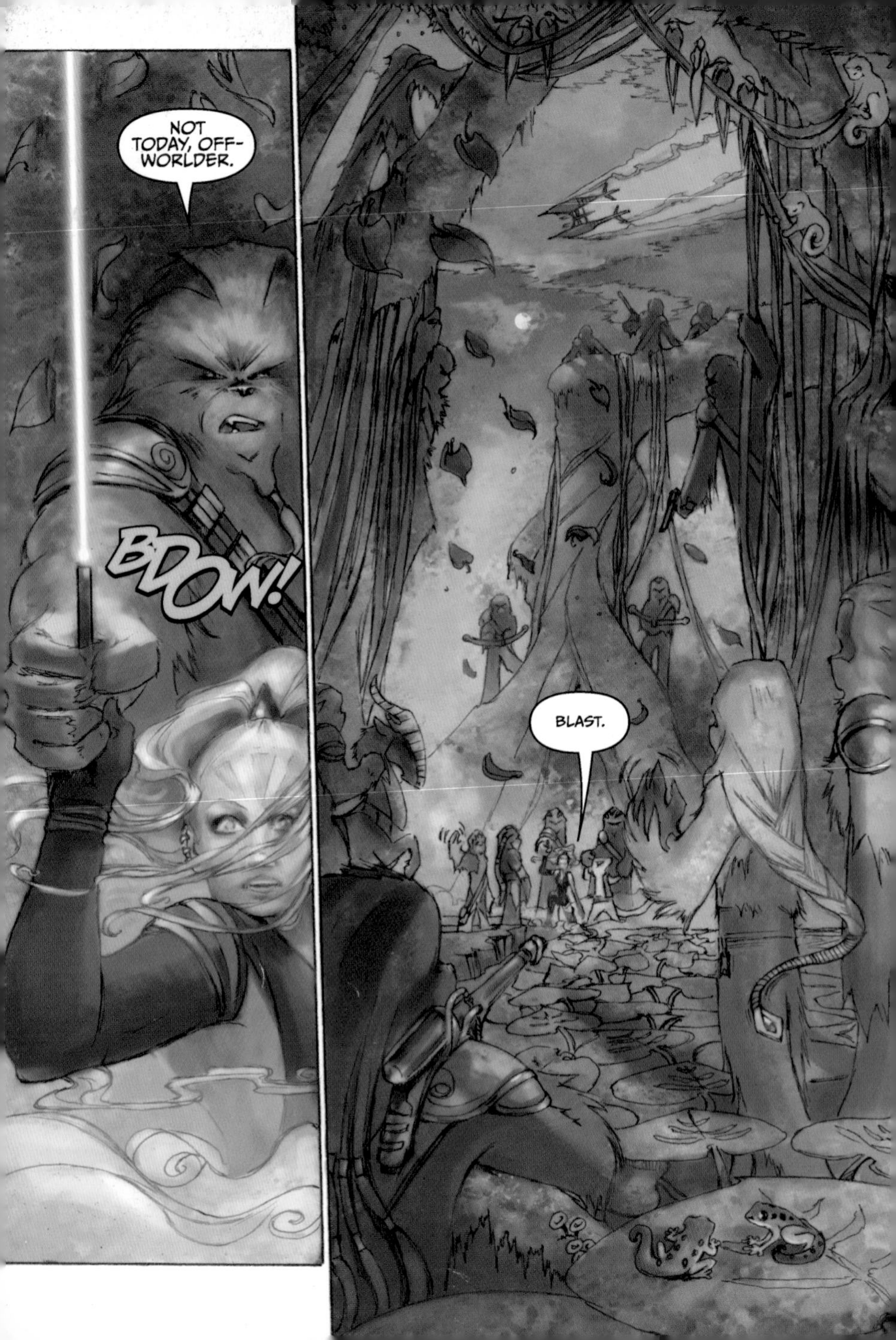
NOT TODAY, OFF-WORLDER.
BDOW!
BLAST.

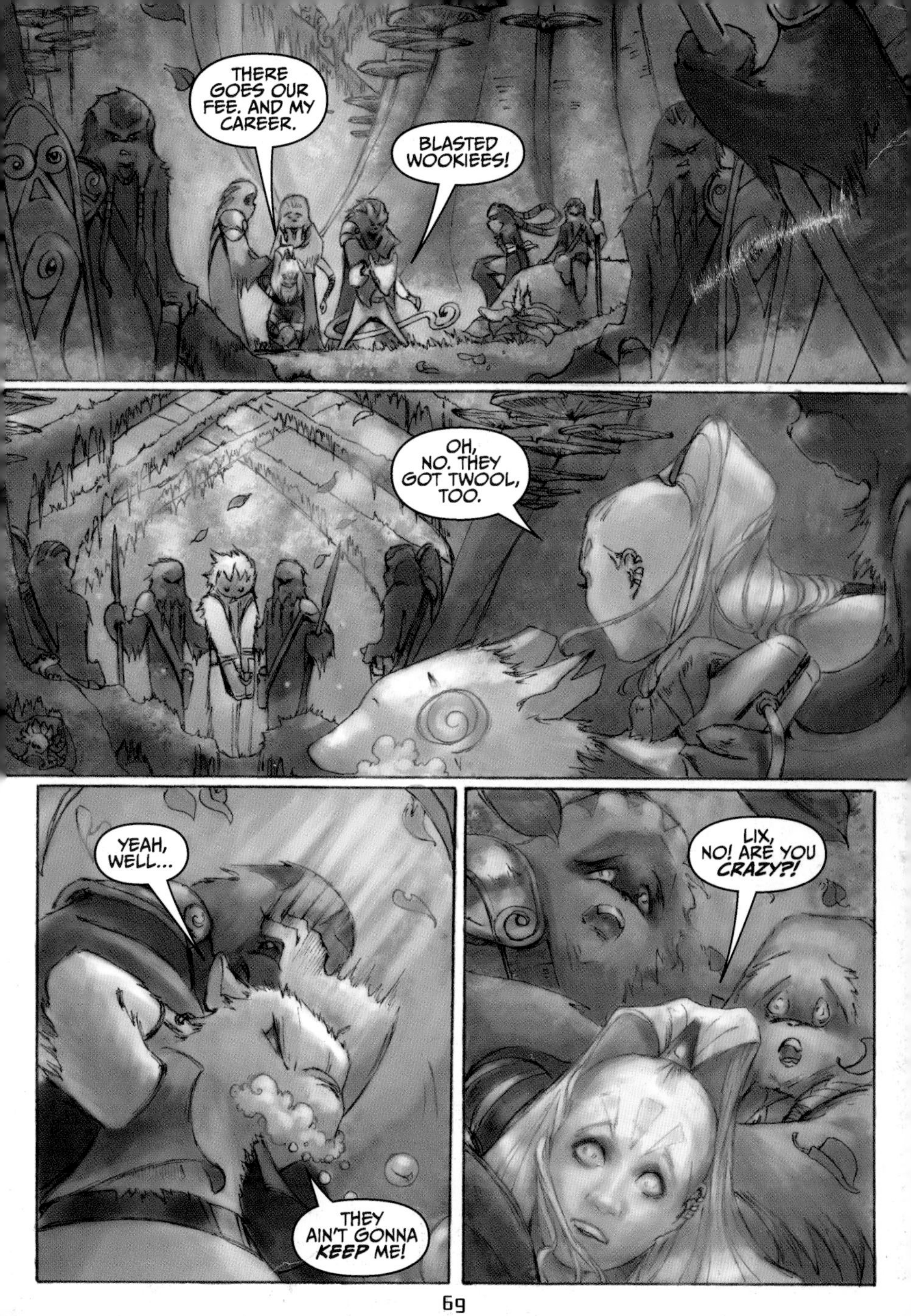
THERE GOES OUR FEE. AND MY CAREER.
BLASTED WOOKIEES!
OH, NO. THEY GOT TWOOL, TOO.
YEAH, WELL...
THEY AIN'T GONNA **KEEP** ME!
LIX, NO! ARE YOU **CRAZY?!**

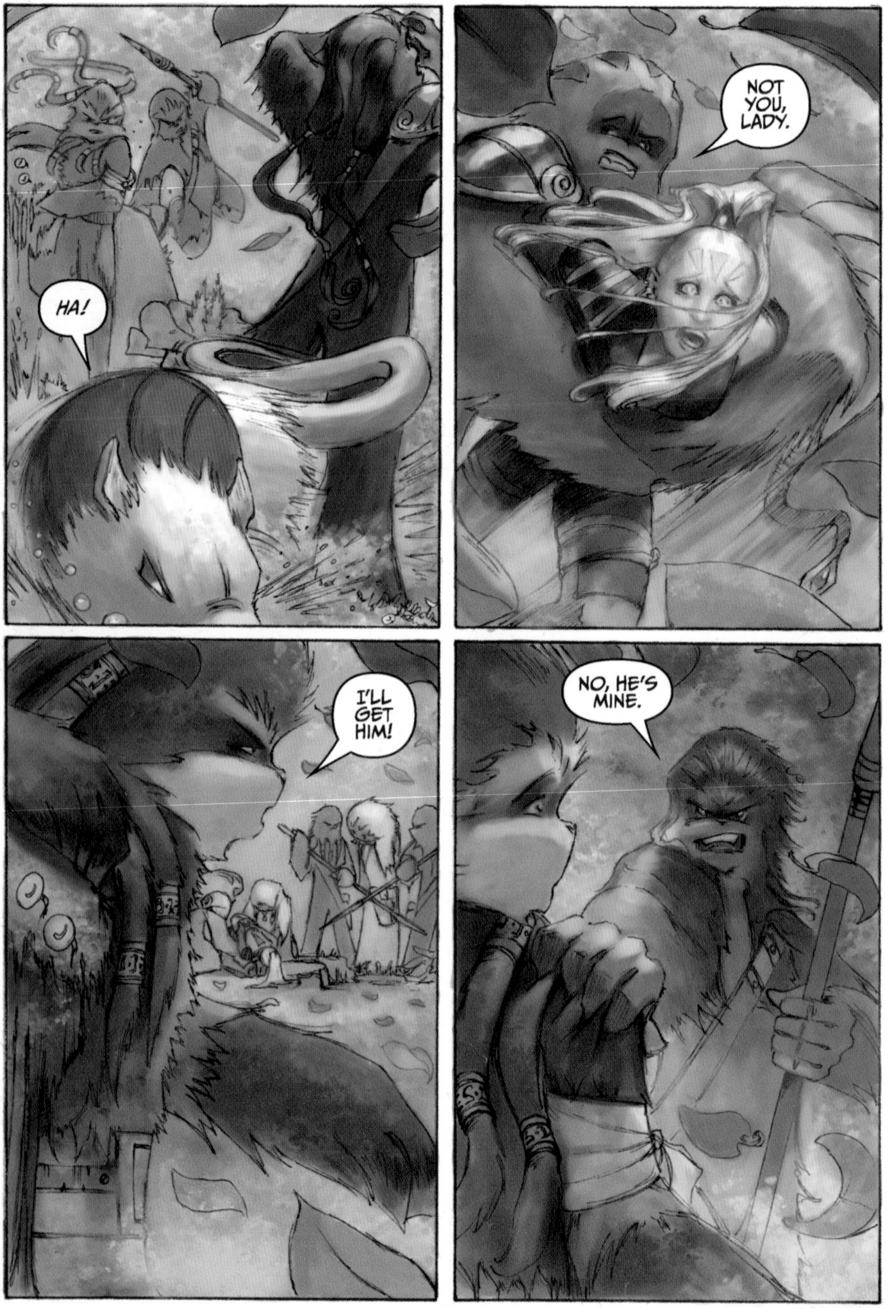
HA!
NOT YOU, LADY.
I'LL GET HIM!
NO, HE'S MINE.

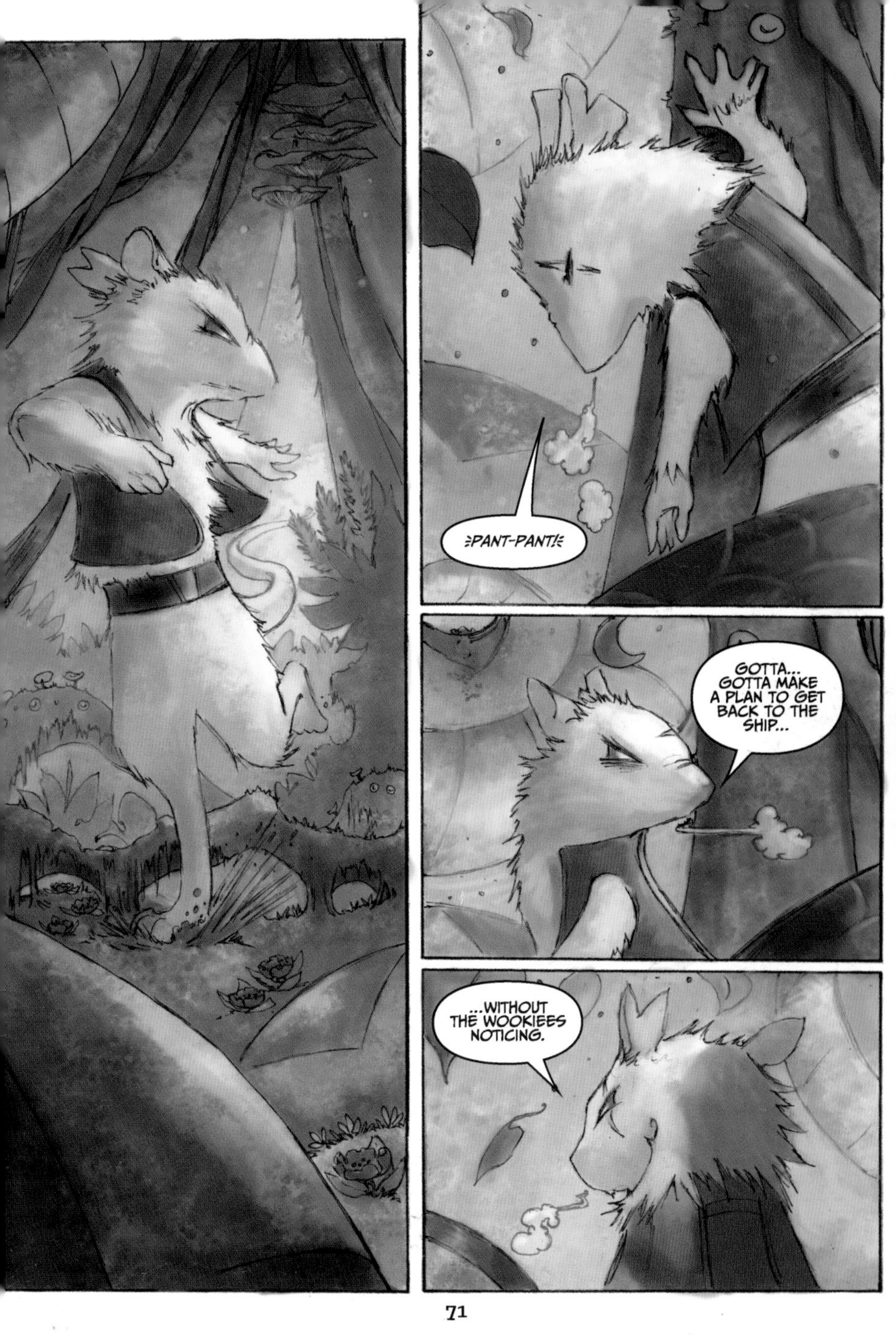

=PANT-PANT!=
GOTTA... GOTTA MAKE A PLAN TO GET BACK TO THE SHIP...
...WITHOUT THE WOOKIEES NOTICING.

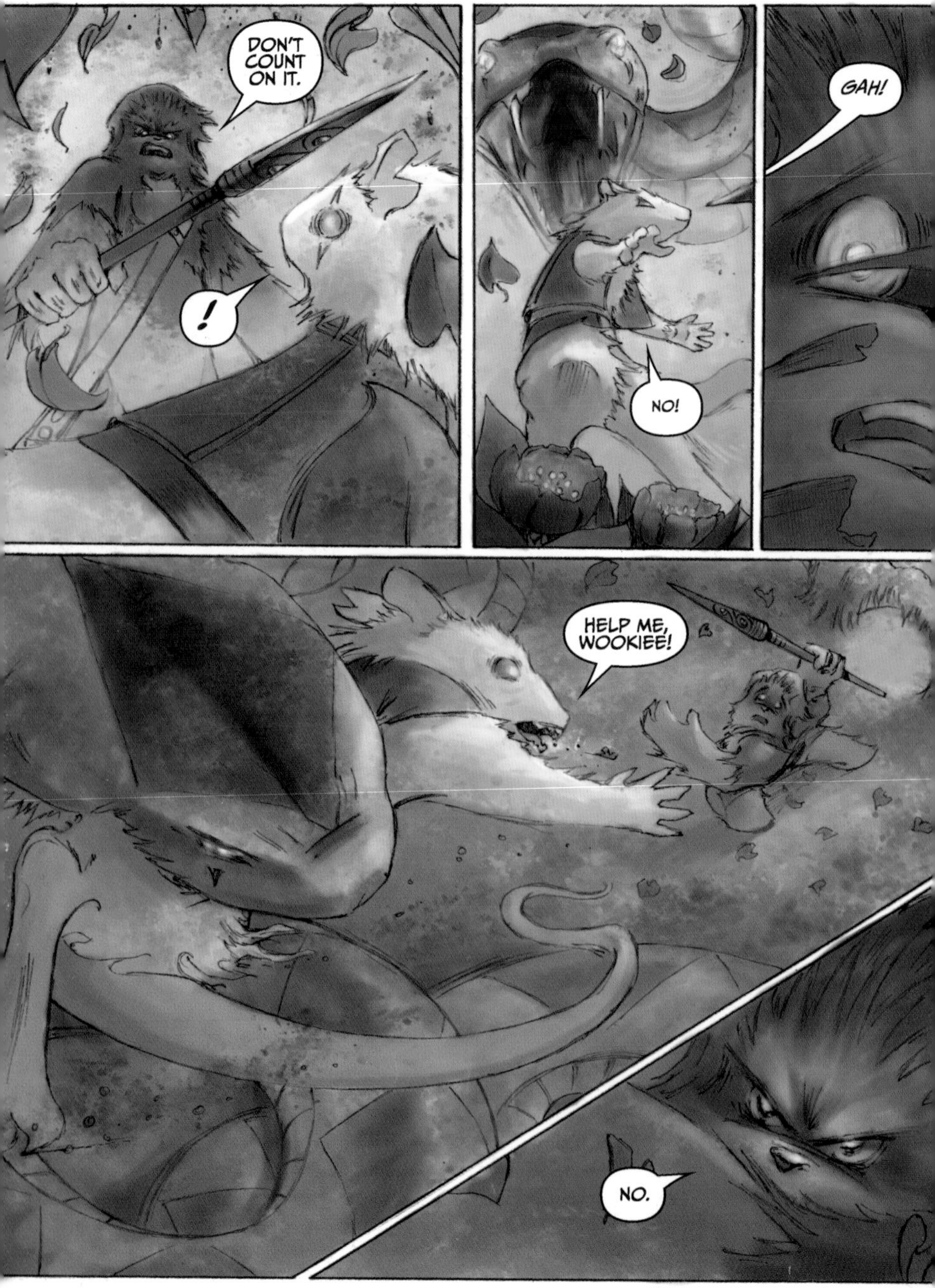
DON'T COUNT ON IT.
!
NO!
GAH!
HELP ME, WOOKIEE!
NO.

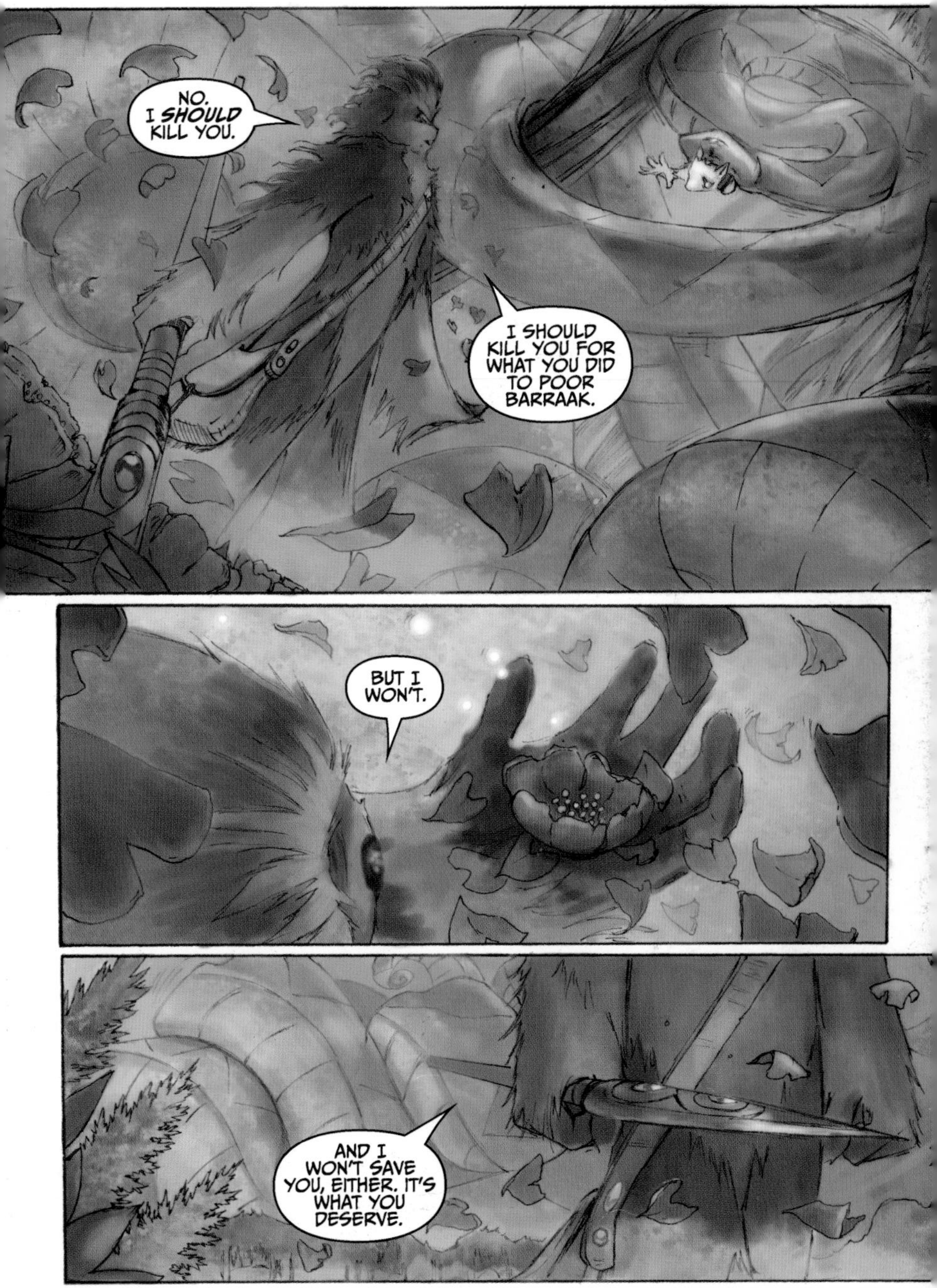
NO. I *SHOULD* KILL YOU.
I SHOULD KILL YOU FOR WHAT YOU DID TO POOR BARRAAK.
BUT I WON'T.
AND I WON'T SAVE YOU, EITHER. IT'S WHAT YOU DESERVE.

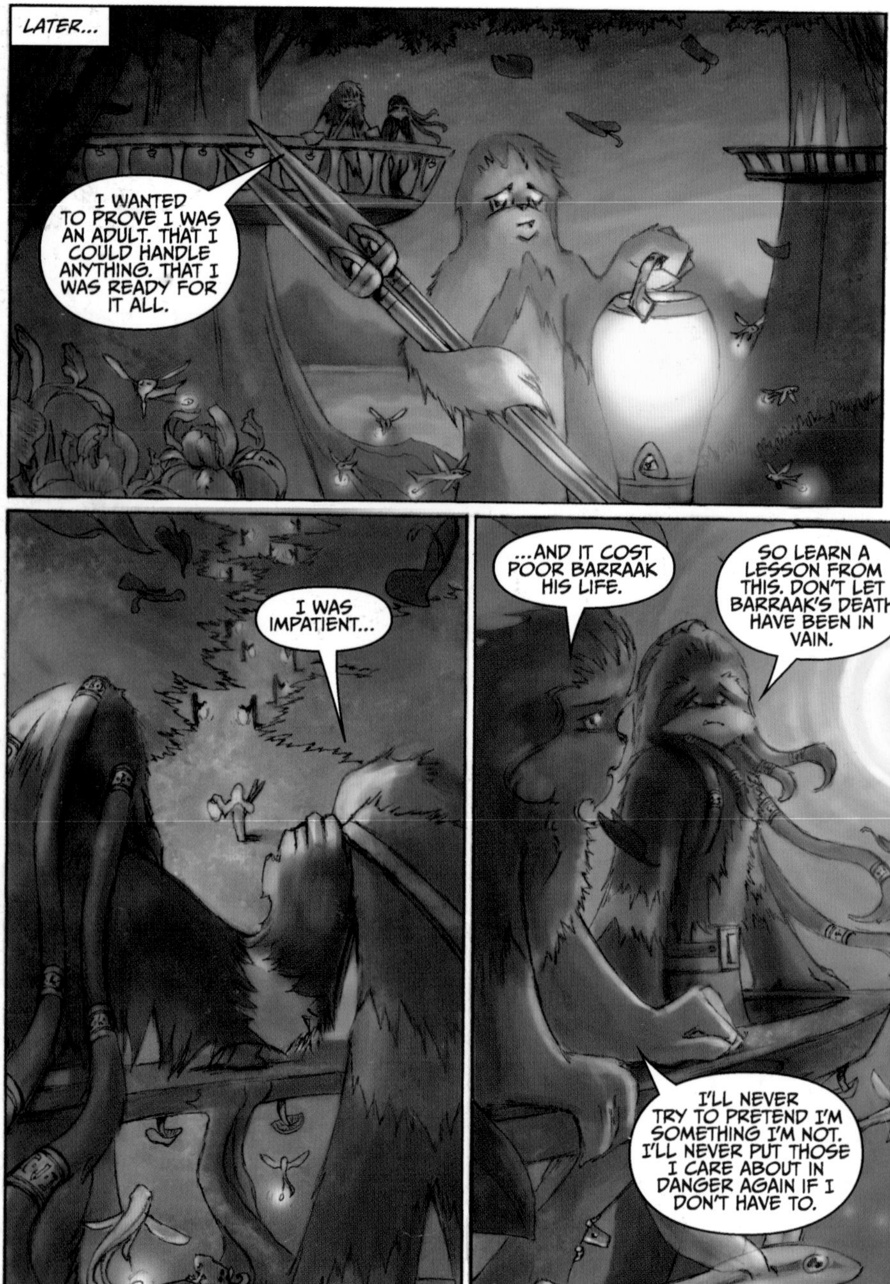
LATER...
I WANTED TO PROVE I WAS AN ADULT. THAT I COULD HANDLE ANYTHING. THAT I WAS READY FOR IT ALL.
I WAS IMPATIENT...
...AND IT COST POOR BARRAAK HIS LIFE.
SO LEARN A LESSON FROM THIS. DON'T LET BARRAAK'S DEATH HAVE BEEN IN VAIN.
I'LL NEVER TRY TO PRETEND I'M SOMETHING I'M NOT. I'LL NEVER PUT THOSE I CARE ABOUT IN DANGER AGAIN IF I DON'T HAVE TO.

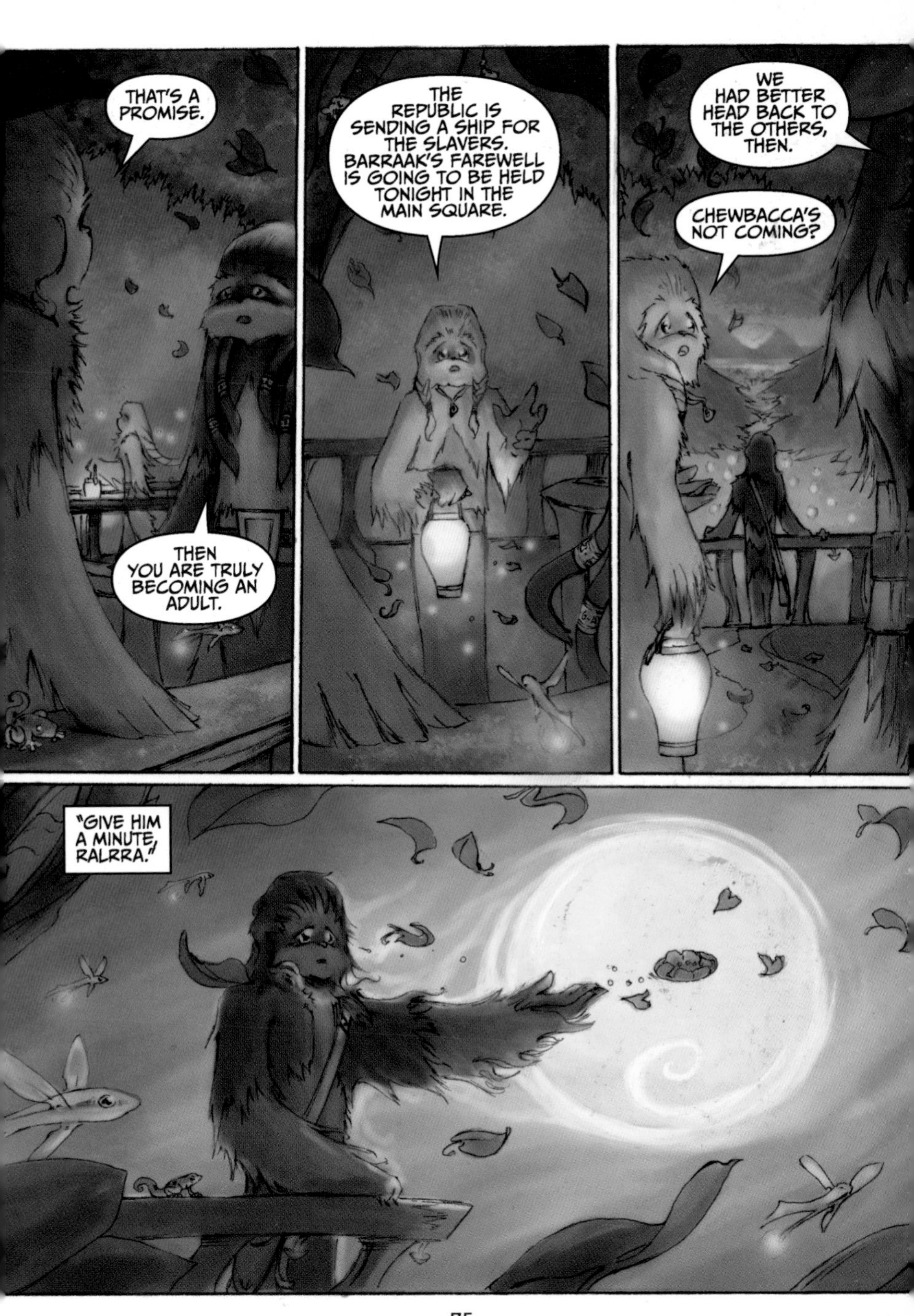
THAT'S A PROMISE.
THEN YOU ARE TRULY BECOMING AN ADULT.
THE REPUBLIC IS SENDING A SHIP FOR THE SLAVERS. BARRAAK'S FAREWELL IS GOING TO BE HELD TONIGHT IN THE MAIN SQUARE.
WE HAD BETTER HEAD BACK TO THE OTHERS, THEN.
CHEWBACCA'S NOT COMING?
"GIVE HIM A MINUTE, RALRRA."

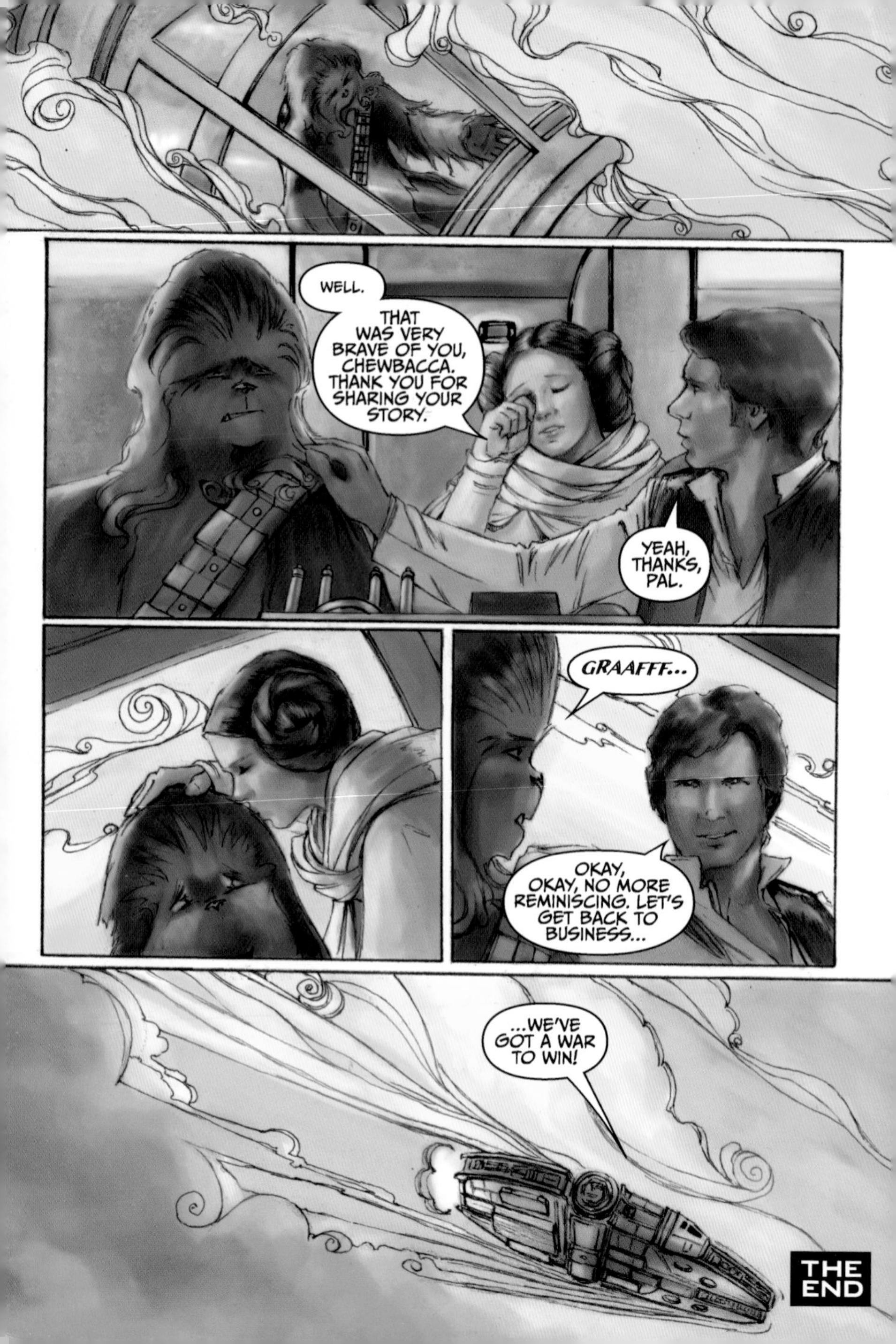
WELL.
THAT WAS VERY BRAVE OF YOU, CHEWBACCA. THANK YOU FOR SHARING YOUR STORY.
YEAH, THANKS, PAL.
GRAAFFF...
OKAY, OKAY, NO MORE REMINISCING. LET'S GET BACK TO BUSINESS...
...WE'VE GOT A WAR TO WIN!
THE END

President and Publisher **Mike Richardson**

Executive Vice President **Neil Hankerson**

Chief Financial Officer **Tom Weddle**

Vice President of Publishing **Randy Stradley**

Vice President of Book Trade Sales **Michael Martens**

Vice President of Business Affairs **Anita Nelson**

Vice President of Marketing **Micha Hershman**

Vice President of Product Development **David Scroggy**

Vice President of Information Technology **Dale LaFountain**

Senior Director of Print, Design, and Production **Darlene Vogel**

General Counsel **Ken Lizzi**

Director of Scheduling **Cara Niece**

Senior Managing Editor **Scott Allie**

Senior Books Editor **Chris Warner**

Executive Editor **Diana Schutz**

Director of Print and Development **Cary Grazzini**

Art Director **Lia Ribacchi**

Editorial Director **Davey Estrada**

STAR WARS GRAPHIC NOVEL TIMELINE (IN YEARS)

Omnibus: Tales of the Jedi—5,000–3,986 BSW4

Knights of the Old Republic—3,964–3,963 BSW4

The Old Republic—3653, 3678 BSW4

Knight Errant—1,032 BSW4

Jedi vs. Sith—1,000 BSW4

Omnibus: Rise of the Sith—33 BSW4

Episode I: The Phantom Menace—32 BSW4

Omnibus: Emissaries and Assassins—32 BSW4

Twilight—31 BSW4

Omnibus: Menace Revealed—31–22 BSW4

Darkness—30 BSW4

The Stark Hyperspace War—30 BSW4

Rite of Passage—28 BSW4

Honor and Duty—22 BSW4

Blood Ties—22 BSW4

Episode II: Attack of the Clones—22 BSW4

Clone Wars—22–19 BSW4

Clone Wars Adventures—22–19 BSW4

General Grievous—22–19 BSW4

Episode III: Revenge of the Sith—19 BSW4

Dark Times—19 BSW4

Omnibus: Droids—5.5 BSW4

Boba Fett: Enemy of the Empire—3 BSW4

Underworld—1 BSW4

Episode IV: A New Hope—SW4

Classic Star Wars—0–3 ASW4

A Long Time Ago . . .—0–4 ASW4

Empire—0 ASW4

Rebellion—0 ASW4

Boba Fett: Man with a Mission—0 ASW4

Omnibus: Early Victories—0–3 ASW4

Jabba the Hutt: The Art of the Deal—1 ASW4

Episode V: The Empire Strikes Back—3 ASW4

Omnibus: Shadows of the Empire—3.5–4.5 ASW4

Episode VI: Return of the Jedi—4 ASW4

Omnibus: X-Wing Rogue Squadron—4–5 ASW4

Heir to the Empire—9 ASW4

Dark Force Rising—9 ASW4

The Last Command—9 ASW4

Dark Empire—10 ASW4

Boba Fett: Death, Lies, and Treachery—10 ASW4

Crimson Empire—11 ASW4

Jedi Academy: Leviathan—12 ASW4

Union—19 ASW4

Chewbacca—25 ASW4

Invasion—25 ASW4

Legacy—130–137 ASW4

Old Republic Era
25,000 – 1000 years before
Star Wars: A New Hope

Rise of the Empire Era
1000 – 0 years before
Star Wars: A New Hope

Rebellion Era
0 – 5 years after
Star Wars: A New Hope

New Republic Era
5 – 25 years after
Star Wars: A New Hope

New Jedi Order Era
25+ years after
Star Wars: A New Hope

Legacy Era
130+ years after
Star Wars: A New Hope

Vector
Crosses four eras in the timeline

Volume 1
Knights of the Old Republic Volume 5
Dark Times Volume 3

Volume 2
Rebellion Volume 4
Legacy Volume 6

BSW4 = before *Episode IV: A New Hope*. ASW4 = after *Episode IV: A New Hope*.